Parenting a Teen or Young Adult with Asperger Syndrome (Autistic Spectrum Disorder)

by the same author

Parenting a Child with Asperger Syndrome
200 Tips and Strategies
ISBN 978 1 84310 137 6
eISBN 978 1 84642 420 5

Appreciating Asperger Syndrome
Looking at the Upside – with 300 Positive Points
Foreword by Kenneth Hall
ISBN 978 1 84310 625 8
eISBN 978 1 84642 913 2

of related interest

Asperger Syndrome, the Universe and Everything
Kenneth's Book
Kenneth Hall
ISBN 978 1 85302 930 1
eISBN 978 1 84642 699 5

Asperger's Syndrome
A Guide for Parents and Professionals
Tony Attwood
Foreword by Lorna Wing
ISBN 978 1 85302 577 8
eISBN 978 1 84642 697 1

Freaks, Geeks and Asperger Syndrome
A User Guide to Adolescence
Luke Jackson
Foreword by Tony Attwood
ISBN 978 1 84310 098 0
eISBN 978 1 84642 356 7

Asperger's Syndrome – That Explains Everything
Strategies for Education, Life and Just About Everything Else
Stephen Bradshaw
Foreword by Francesca Happé
ISBN 978 1 84905 351 8
eISBN 978 0 85700 702 5

Parenting
a TEEN or
YOUNG ADULT
with Asperger
Syndrome

(AUTISTIC SPECTRUM DISORDER)

325 Ideas, Insights, Tips and Strategies

BRENDA BOYD

Jessica Kingsley *Publishers*
London and Philadelphia

First published in 2014
by Jessica Kingsley Publishers
73 Collier Street
London N1 9BE, UK
and
400 Market Street, Suite 400
Philadelphia, PA 19106, USA

www.jkp.com

Library of Congress Cataloging in Publication Data
Boyd, Brenda.
Parenting a teen or young adult with Asperger syndrome
(autism spectrum disorder) : 325 ideas,
insights, tips and strategies / Brenda Boyd.
pages cm
ISBN 978-1-84905-282-5 (alk. paper)
1. Asperger's syndrome in adolescence. 2. Parent and child. 3. Parenting. I. Title.
HQ773.8.B68 2014
618.92'858832--dc23
2013030412

British Library Cataloguing in Publication Data
A CIP catalogue record for this book is available from the British Library

ISBN 978 1 84905 282 5
eISBN 978 0 85700 587 8

Printed and bound in Great Britain by Bell & Bain Ltd, Glasgow

*I would like to thank a few people who really matter to me
and who have supported me through thick and thin:*

Bap Kennedy

Christine Elliott

Kenneth Hall

Lily and Jim Kennedy

Dee Harding

Contents

INTRODUCTION   9

About the book   10

Parents and other pivotal people   11

1. SOME THINGS NEVER CHANGE   15

The greatest need   15

Looking after yourself   17

2. UNDERSTANDING ASPERGER ADOLESCENCE   21

Understanding is crucial   21

The work of understanding   26

3. THE SEVEN KEY INSIGHTS   33

Key Insight # 1: Asperger extremes   34

Key Insight # 2: Fish out of water   38

Key Insight # 3: Rates of development   44

Key Insight # 4: Processing and sensory differences   49

Key Insight # 5: Mind blindness   55

Key Insight # 6: Rigidity   60

Key Insight # 7: Social vulnerability   65

4. THE BEST APPROACH   73

Being calm and assertive   74

Parenting with confidence   76

Being pragmatic   80

Encouraging motivation   85

Avoiding conflict   88

5. YOUR RELATIONSHIP WITH YOUR CHILD   95

Being on the same side   96

Giving him the benefit of the doubt   100

Mutual respect   104

6. SELF-IMAGE   109
Encourage him to have a positive self-regard   *110*
Encourage him to have a positive attitude to Asperger
   Syndrome   *114*
Help shape core beliefs   *118*

7. COMMUNICATION THAT WORKS   125
Ready to listen, ready to talk   *126*
Clear, honest and direct communication   *131*

8. A PREDICTABLE WORLD?   137
Understanding control versus chaos   *138*
Encouraging order and structure   *142*
Setting boundaries and limits   *148*

9. THE PROBLEM WITH PEOPLE   153
The Social Curriculum   *154*
Emotions and nonverbal communication   *167*
Positive social experiences   *175*

10. PREPARATION FOR ADULTHOOD   181
Encouraging self-awareness and responsibility   *182*
Thinking about college and career   *189*
Encouraging a positive outlook   *194*

11. WHEN THINGS GO OFF THE RAILS   197
Depression   *198*
Challenging and destructive behaviour   *204*

TIP FINDER: A LIST OF ALL THE IDEAS, INSIGHTS, TIPS AND
STRATEGIES IN THE ORDER THAT THEY APPEAR THROUGHOUT
THE BOOK   213

USEFUL WEBSITES   229

BIBLIOGRAPHY   231

INDEX   233

Introduction

It is about ten years since I wrote my first book, *Parenting A Child With Asperger Syndrome*. My son, Kenneth, has Asperger Syndrome (AS) and he was the inspiration behind the book. When I wrote it he was 12 years old and just about to enter adolescence. Today he is 23 – so not a child anymore! And there has been, as you can imagine, a lot of water under the bridge in the meantime.

Over the years from time to time I thought about writing a follow up to the original book, but I had a lot of reservations and I kept procrastinating. I didn't want anyone to think I was holding myself up as some kind of parenting model because, I have to admit it, the journey through his adolescent years was a tough one – for him and for me. And I know I made a lot of mistakes.

That's only natural of course, for we all make mistakes. And it's only by looking at them that we can learn from them. But when I look back now some pretty dark times come to mind – times I'd rather forget really – when I found it hard to cope, when I despaired for Kenneth and for the future and when things seemed bleak and daunting. At our lowest point, I actually put Kenneth out of the house and sent him to live with his father because I honestly couldn't put up with him anymore… But that's another story!

Anyway here's the good news. All those problems are in the past now. It's a fantastic relief to be finally at the point where we can look back and laugh. We made it through in the end! I'm in a much better place than ever now and so is he.

So if your child is going through a difficult adolescence you need to know there is hope, and that it won't last forever. There is light at the end of the tunnel, even though it can be hard to believe that when you're still in the middle of the tunnel.

Kenneth will always have AS of course, and it will always impact his life. I have never thought in terms of trying to get rid of his AS or 'cure' him of it, because Aspergers is part of who he is. It's as simple as that.

Yes it's probably true that if he didn't have Aspergers life would be easier for him – and for me! It's easy to imagine that without AS Kenneth might have done something more conventional with his life by now – perhaps got some impressive qualification and a 'good job'. But if I try to picture Kenneth without Asperger Syndrome, it is a different person that I picture. And here's the truth – I don't want him to be a different person and, thank heavens, neither does he.

But Kenneth is one of those Aspies who rarely does anything unless he either really wants to do it or sees a good point in it. So what's he up to these days? For now he is pursuing his interest in music, and he is playing guitar in a classic rock band. As to the future, who knows – anything is possible. He has his own story, but that is not what this book is about. If he ever decides to tell it, maybe he will write another book himself some day. That's up to him.

But for me the bottom line is this – Kenneth is a young adult now and for the most part he has turned out happy and well. He and I get along very well with each other these days and I am very glad he is in my life. And that, to me as a parent, is success.

ABOUT THE BOOK
Extreme parenting

In many ways Asperger Syndrome is a condition that is all about extremes, and as a result Asperger parenting can be like some extreme form of parenting – at times extremely challenging and at times extremely rewarding. And this is especially true when your child reaches adolescence. So, in many respects, the kind of parenting that works best for a young person with Asperger Syndrome is a larger than life version of what will work best for any other young person.

Note on language

I refer to people with Asperger Syndrome as male (he/him/his) throughout the book. It is true that there are more males than females diagnosed with Asperger Syndrome, but that is not the reason. It is just a matter of convenience – it is easier to say 'him' each time than 'him or her' and I thought it might be confusing to keep alternating. But the tips are meant to apply to males and females.

Sometimes I refer to teenagers and adolescents as young people and sometimes as children, because as parents we always think of our sons and daughters as our children, even when they are adults.

Finally, I refer to Asperger Syndrome and people with Asperger Syndrome in various ways, for example AS, Aspies, and so on.

I hope none of these terms cause any offence.

The tips

This book is organised so that all the ideas, tips and strategies run through the main text and are then repeated in list format at the back, in the Tip Finder.

It is good to be open to trying new ideas, but if any of the ideas and tips don't make intuitive sense to you, just let them go – at least for the moment. Trust your own judgement. You know your child best!

If you read the book from start to finish, hopefully one point should lead to the next in such a way that the reasoning behind each of the tips makes sense. But if you are looking for an idea quickly you can go straight to the Tip Finder at the end of the book.

PARENTS AND OTHER PIVOTAL PEOPLE

First things first – this book is not just meant for parents. It is for anyone who wants to understand and help a young person who has AS. As parents naturally we have a pivotal role to play in the lives of our children, but sometimes other people can be pivotal too. And we recognize *pivotal people* when they come along, for when you have a child or children with AS you develop a kind of antenna that helps you know these things.

Pivotal people stand out as significant figures in our children's lives. They make a real, positive and lasting difference, and they come in many shapes and sizes. Often they are family members (particularly grandparents), but they can also be friends or neighbours. And sometimes people with a professional involvement in our children's lives can turn out to be pivotal too: for example teachers, social workers, tutors, etc. We recognise them when we see them go the extra mile, and when we see the benefits of their involvement in our child's life.

Pivotal people are important for various reasons. One is that they can be a great practical help. For, as we all know, when there is a child or children in the family with AS it can put a strain on the whole family. So it can mean a lot to have someone on the team, so to speak, who is willing to lend a helping hand. And if he or she also gets on well with other members of the family and brings along some fresh, positive energy as well as some moral support, then that's an added bonus. But the most important contribution that parents and pivotal people make comes as a result of their relationship with our children.

When our children reach adolescence, we can't help worrying about them. We are very tuned in to their difficulties and vulnerability because we know how out of step they are with their peers, and we know that during adolescence this situation is likely to become even more extreme. One of our main concerns is that they might become isolated and depressed. For we know that adolescents can be intolerant of other adolescents who do not fit in. And we know that outsiders often judge or avoid our children when they don't like or approve of their behaviour, or when it makes them uncomfortable. But pivotal people are different in that respect. Pivotal people are committed, yes. But, more than that, they believe in our children and find them engaging, endearing and interesting.

Ideally whenever a problem arises, as it inevitably will, pivotal people deal with it in an honest and straightforward manner. Hopefully they resolve it in a positive way, so that lessons have been learned all round. Pivotal people regard our children's unique quirks and unusual approach to life as refreshing. In short, they like our children – and that means a lot!

So why does this book have the word 'parenting' in the title if it is aimed more widely? For a few reasons really. The most obvious one is that it is meant as a follow on from my original book, *Parenting a Child with Asperger Syndrome*. But it is also because as parents, generally speaking, we have the most significant role to play in our children's lives – if only because we are there for the longest time, and are more involved than any of the other people who come in and out of their lives.

But mainly this book is written from a parent's perspective because I am a parent myself! Looking back on my adult life, I have had quite a varied career really. For example, I started off as a lawyer and have ended up as a bass guitar player in my husband's band, which plays in various different countries around the world. And along the way I have had a variety of other jobs and roles: I have worked in a government post, in a hospice and for an autism charity, as well as dabbling in song writing, painting and, of course, writing. But of all the jobs I have done, the most important by far is being a parent and I would hate to lose sight of that.

If you are reading this book and you are not a parent of a child with Aspergers, then I take my hat off to you. I imagine there must be at least one young person in your life who has the condition – and that person must be important to you. Perhaps you are a grandparent or step-parent. Maybe a teacher or friend. It doesn't really matter. In fact young people with AS ideally do better with a wide network of good people in their lives. Such a network should include their parents of course, but other people can play a pivotal role too.

I know that for certain from my own personal experience because I have seen the part my husband, Bap, has played in the life of my son, Kenneth. Bap only came into our lives about six years ago when Kenneth was 17. But as Kenneth's step-father, he has made an extremely powerful and positive difference. I am deeply grateful to him for that (and so is Kenneth, he asked me to say!).

I wanted to tell you this at the outset, because for me Bap is living proof that you don't need to be a biological mother or father, or any kind of blood relation, to play a pivotal role in the life of a young person with AS. Simply by caring, trying to understand and becoming involved, you can help make the world an easier, more comfortable place for him.

1

Some Things Never Change

The greatest need
Looking after yourself

THE GREATEST NEED

'The greatest need that any child has is the need for
unconditional love.' (Boyd 2003)

That was the central message of my original book, and it is the central
message of this one too, so in a way you could say that some things
never change!

As parents, we know about the power of unconditional love. Our
number one parenting task is not only to love our children but to
make sure they know at a deep level that they are loved and accepted
for exactly who they are. This is the foundation upon which our
parenting is laid but, when your child has Asperger Syndrome, it can
be hard to get this basic foundation laid. And all this is no less true
when our children reach adolescence.

So, if the central message of this book is the same as the original,
what are the differences?

Well, for one thing, I am ten years older and hopefully a bit
wiser, and I have tried to pass on some things that it has taken ten
more years to learn! And for another, life tends to become more
complicated at this stage, so our number one parenting task can
become more challenging.

For example, adolescents do not like to be patronised, so we need to adapt our approach in subtle ways to take this into account. Some of the strategies that worked when our children were small may become redundant as they grow older, and we need a range of new ones. As they grow and mature, the emphasis needs to shift. Ultimately they want to be in charge of their own lives, and there are a lot of things we can do at this stage to help prepare and equip them for adulthood.

Usually by the time children with AS reach adolescence they have accumulated more than their fair share of experiences of 'getting it wrong'. Even if they have got to this age without getting a diagnosis, they usually have some kind of feeling that they don't quite 'fit in'. They have probably made plenty of social gaffes and are likely to feel out on a limb and at odds with the world. A lot of emphasis will probably have been put on trying to get them to modify and improve certain aspects of their behaviour, and other people may have reacted to them in a negative way. Presumably, at some point they have been diagnosed with AS and, even if this has been handled with great skill and sensitivity, it is likely that this has affected their confidence. For all these reasons it is more crucial now than ever that we love them unconditionally and do our best to help them feel loved.

LOOKING AFTER YOURSELF

My original book started with a section on looking after yourself, and ten years on I am more convinced than ever that this section needs to come first. For when your child has AS, your role as parent is very important and very demanding, and this becomes even more true when they are going through adolescence. So, even if you have read the original book, or if you don't think you need to read this, at least have a skim through the tips in this chapter before going on to the next one!

TIP BOX

Looking after yourself

1   Keep your batteries charged up
2   Talking helps
3   Get support
4   Don't neglect other areas of your life
5   Worry less, plan more
6   Let yourself off the hook

1 Keep your batteries charged up

We all get busy and tired from time to time; and when our children reach adolescence life can become very challenging. But if we keep overdoing things we can end up run down and exhausted. Think about your mobile phone. If you let it run out of charge it becomes useless, so you know to keep an eye on the charge level and make sure this doesn't happen. And your own energy is just the same – you cannot function properly when your batteries are drained.

Remember, there is no point in letting yourself get burned out, and it is not selfish to look after yourself. When you are rested you can think more clearly and do a much better parenting job. So make a point of keeping your batteries charged up in whatever way works best for you. That may mean you need to go off on a short break, go to the gym, or for a walk, or listen to some music...or it may be something simple like having a coffee with a friend.

2 Talking helps

Make friends with other parents of children with AS. We have so much in common and can learn so much just from talking to each other. So develop mutually supportive friendships. Look on the internet, join parent groups... Do whatever it takes to help you feel connected and supported and know that you are not alone.

3 Get support

Find out what practical and financial support is available and figure out how it might be of help to you, your child with Asperger Syndrome, or your family.

Make the most of any help that is available – from friends, family, professional and charitable bodies and any source you can think of. The National Autistic Society is a good starting point for resources and support (see the Useful Websites section for details).

4 Don't neglect other areas of your life

Adolescent children with Asperger Syndrome can cause a lot of worry and take up a lot of your time and energy – so much so that they can end up taking over your life if you are not careful. Try to keep a balance by setting time aside for your other hobbies, interests and relationships.

5 Worry less, plan more

It is very natural to worry from time to time, because you want the best for your child and you are very aware of his problems. Plus you know he faces extra difficulties at this age as a result of his Asperger Syndrome. But remember, worry is worse than useless.

Look squarely at the things that are worrying you. If it is helpful, write down your concerns and your very worst fears and then start making plans. Aim to have a range of strategies, whether from this book or anywhere else, that you can draw upon, which will help you move forward to find solutions and deal with day-to-day difficulties. You will never be able to solve every problem, but you can make a plan, and you can take some steps to head things in the right direction. And that's a good place to start!

6 Let yourself off the hook

Don't give yourself a hard time when you feel you have fallen short. Nobody is perfect and we all make mistakes.

2

Understanding Asperger Adolescence

Understanding is crucial
The work of understanding

The following chapter looks at the benefits of trying to understand your child and suggests ways in which you can try to understand:

- The condition of Asperger Syndrome (Tips 9, 10, 12, 15, 17 and 18)

- The experience of adolescence (Tip 11)

- Your child as an individual, taking into account the impact of Asperger Syndrome and adolescence in his life (Tips 13 and 14)

UNDERSTANDING IS CRUCIAL

We all like to feel understood – there's no doubt about that! The feeling of being misjudged and misunderstood by the world can be a horrible, lonely one. But unfortunately this is a common feeling during adolescence. And we were all adolescents once, so we should have some idea of what this feels like.

If you think back to your own adolescence you might remember times when you felt misunderstood and misjudged – perhaps by your parents. This kind of experience is not unusual. It seems to be part of the teenage angst that is so common at this stage of life. Adolescence can feel like a bit of a no man's land throughout which you are no longer a child, but not yet an adult. During the years of transition, it is natural for young people to question the world and feel at odds with it because they are starting to search for their own identity, truths and values. Inevitably there will be times when they resent some of the ideas, values and people associated with their upbringing and at these times they may feel the need to reject and withdraw from their family and, especially, from their parents.

Misunderstanding and conflict between parents and teenage children is nothing new of course. It seems to have been going on since the days of the Roman Empire (Garland 1991)! During adolescence the relationship between parent and child often suffers, and it may even break down for a while. But generally parents understand that this is all part of a natural process and make allowances to some extent. They expect difficulties, but they reassure themselves that these times of conflict and misunderstanding will come to an end eventually. In the meantime the younger generation find a substitute sense of belonging among their peer group.

If you think back to your own adolescence, you might remember other feelings as well as feelings of being misunderstood and misjudged. Perhaps when you listened to certain music, or associated with certain people, that gave you a powerful sense of belonging. You may remember forming close connections and relationships with your peers, which led to some of the feelings of exhilaration that are also associated with adolescence.

All this is how it normally works anyway. But when you have Asperger Syndrome it's a different story. Yes, you have that natural drive towards autonomy and independent identity, like anyone else. And, yes, you may end up at odds with your parents, like anyone else. But your situation is infinitely more complex and difficult, for various reasons, above all because you probably do not have a peer group to turn to for that substitute sense of belonging. And that means you can end up very alone and isolated.

Usually parents don't expect to understand their children very well while they are going through adolescence. In fact, problems due to misunderstanding seem to be almost an unwritten rule! But we try not to worry about it; we reassure ourselves that it's just a phase, so hopefully it doesn't matter too much.

When our children with Asperger Syndrome go through adolescence, the situation is very different. They may be at their most baffling, maddening and uncommunicative at this age; however, they need our understanding more than ever now. Understanding may be far from easy, but it is well worth making the effort. The following headings summarise some of the benefits that come with understanding:

Demystification!

Aspie behaviour can sometimes seem strange and leave us mystified. Understanding Asperger Syndrome can sometimes help clear up the mystery of strange or difficult behaviour.

'To understand is to forgive'

Generally speaking it is worth trying to understand other people because sometimes we judge harshly that which we don't understand.

Predictability

A deep understanding of AS can give us a masterful insight into the factors which are likely to influence and determine an Aspie's behaviour – and sometimes being able to predict behaviour can be as important as being able to control it. For example:

- When you understand your child, you are in a better position to predict what he is likely to do or not do. You are less likely to be taken aback by his behaviours and reactions. And you are in a better position to plan how to respond.

- You know what's reasonable and fair to expect from him and can set the bar just right.

- You are more likely to have insights which can help you figure out the currency which might motivate him to move in the right direction.

Allowances

AS is something of a hidden disorder, and so the world often does not make allowances. People with AS face challenges every day that are not obvious to other people and often their 'problem' behaviour is actually their coping mechanism. But it is hard to make allowances for something you don't really understand. It is therefore more important for us as parents to do so, and we are more likely to make appropriate allowances when we have insight and understanding.

For example, we might want to make allowances for:

- sensory issues
- processing issues
- social difficulties
- mind blindness
- rigidity.

Needs

Through understanding we can better identify and meet needs. We can also help him learn ways to meet his own needs, and this can be an important part of his preparation for adult life.

The best approach

We all want to know the best ways to relate to our children, manage difficulties and generally help them. We can learn this through trial and error, but insight can help us work out our best approach (see also Chapter 4).

Learning

Children with AS often have their own very distinctive learning styles. For example they may be visual learners. And they may learn some things extremely easily and have great difficulties with others. When we know this we can adapt how we teach them and tailor learning style and goals.

Appreciation

Real insight and understanding of another human being, and especially of the challenges they face, generally leads to appreciation, and appreciation is an intrinsic part of love.

Spreading understanding

The more we understand, the better the position we are in to educate, encourage and help others to understand, appreciate and make allowances.

Helping him understand himself

The better we know and understand him, the better we can help him know and understand himself. The right kind of self-awareness will be lacking in judgement and will help him to:

- recognise his own strengths and weaknesses and learn to accept and come to terms with them

- learn to manage his life and relationships better, taking account of his strengths and weaknesses

- recognise his own needs and learn how they can be met.

This in turn can help him feel he is not stupid, inferior or bad, and to feel better about himself generally (see also Chapter 6).

Aspergers can help us learn about ourselves too

As we do the work required to help us understand our children, sometimes we find that we have more in common with them than we realised. We might even come to recognise some Aspergers traits in ourselves! When this happens, it can deepen our understanding of our children and help us relate to them better.

It can lead to an interesting journey!

THE WORK OF UNDERSTANDING

TIP BOX

The work of understanding

7   Resolve to understand
8   Understanding takes time
9   Look at online resources and make contacts
10 Look close to home
11 Roll back the years
12 See AS as a signpost, not a label
13 Listen!
14 Encourage him to open up
15 Look within
16 Help him understand himself
17 Know the Seven Key Insights
18 Become a student

7 Resolve to understand

The work of understanding your child may not be straightforward. It involves looking at the part played by Asperger Syndrome and adolescence in his life, as well as making the effort to understand him as a unique individual. But he needs our understanding more than ever at this time of his life.

Think of a time, during your own adolescence or otherwise, when you felt isolated and misunderstood. If you were lucky enough to find even one person who understood you – or at least who cared enough to try – you may remember what a difference that person made and how much you appreciated him. That person may have played a pivotal role in your life, and you can do the same for your child.

Make it your mission to understand you child. You will be giving him a priceless gift.

8 Understanding takes time

Asperger Syndrome is a notoriously complex condition which even the experts find hard to understand, so it is only realistic to see the task of understanding as a long-term process – probably life-long in fact – and to approach it with an attitude of openness and curiosity. You need to be in for the long haul!

9 Look at online resources and make contacts

These days it is easy to learn about AS online and there are plenty of resources available. Your local autism charity is often a good starting point for resources and support (see the Useful Websites section for details). Additionally you may be able to find a local Asperger group where you can connect with other parents and professionals and compare notes with them.

10 Look close to home

While the 'causes' of AS may be complex and subject to controversy, most experts at least agree that there is a genetic component. So, statistically speaking, there is a good chance that you yourself have some AS traits. It can be helpful to look at these. What are they? How have they affected you in your life and what coping strategies have you developed? And you might be able to see traits in other family members as well.

The advantage of this approach is that it can give you and other family members some real insight into what, in a much more extreme way, your child might be experiencing.

Choose to acknowledge, tune into, accept and get to know the Asperger parts of yourself. When you do so, you will be in a much better position to help your child.

11 Roll back the years

Think back to your own adolescence to give you some insight into the impact that adolescence might be playing in your child's life. This is something we should all be able to understand, because we went through our own adolescence at one point and, even though the world has changed, some things never change.

Depending on your personality and your own personal circumstances, you may remember adolescence as exhilarating and exciting at times. But you may also remember difficult, painful and disappointing times and, unfortunately, it is likely that these memories are closer than the happy ones to what your child is experiencing.

Spend a bit of time trying to recapture the feelings of your own adolescence. Look at old photos. Listen to music that you connected with at the time. If you think back hard enough I'm sure you will remember the intensity of your own teenage angst as well as the joys and thrills.

12 See AS as a signpost, not a label

The AS 'label' can be helpful, but it can also be a clumsy tool. Use it with great sensitivity because your child is a complex individual and AS is only part of who he is. When you see AS as a signpost rather than a label, your child's diagnosis can help to point you in the right direction to understand him better and help him get the help he needs.

13 Listen!

Just as is true for any individual, the best way to understand your child is by meeting him where he is at and truly listening. Look out for the moments when he seems willing to open up to you, and when those moments arise, try to be there and really listen. Do so with respect, humility and an open heart. Listen for what he doesn't say as well as what he does, and try not to make assumptions.

14 Encourage him to open up

Your child may not have a close friend or peer group to relate to or to confide in. If he feels he can open up and talk to at least one person in his life, this can make a great difference to him. You can be that person for him. It may not be easy. It can take a lot of time and patience and he might resist the idea of opening up, especially to parents. If so, don't be disheartened. Think of this as a very long-term but worthwhile goal.

Remember:

- You cannot force him to talk. If you try too hard it can be counter-productive because he may see it as interference and withdraw more.

- Try to create a climate where he feels comfortable to talk and confide.

- Look out for situations and opportunities where he is liable to open up.

- Whenever he does open up and talk to you, aim to respond in such a way that he will want to do it again!

(See Tips 176–185.)

15 Look within

A valuable part of the work of understanding involves looking within – that is, thinking deeply and honestly about your own feelings and experiences in an effort to empathise with your child.

We were all adolescents ourselves once, so we should have at least some understanding about this stage of life. Yes, it's true that times are different today, but human nature doesn't really change and thinking about our own adolescence may yield some valuable insights.

Sometimes when you do look within, you see more clearly than before how much you and your child have in common. Even if you don't have a diagnosis of AS yourself, you may be more alike than you realised. Looking within can help you understand your child, but it may turn out to be the start of a process of self-discovery for you as well!

16 Help him understand himself

Ultimately the goal is that your child comes to understand himself as fully as possible. And that includes understanding Asperger Syndrome and the part that it plays in his life. So part of your job over time is to help your child understand himself, for knowledge is power in this respect, and the better he understands himself the better he will be able to manage and take responsibility for his own life and find his place in the world.

17 Know the Seven Key Insights

AS is a complex and puzzling condition. Things are often not what they seem, but there are certain general key insights which can help unlock the puzzle. We will explore these in Chapter 3, but briefly they are:

1. *Asperger extremes.* 'People with AS are like anyone else, only more so' so it is often possible to gain insight by looking within.

2. *Fish out of water.* People with AS generally feel out of place in the world.

3. *Rates of development.* AS is a developmental disorder. Unless you realise this you can make inappropriate assumptions about his ability and potential, sometimes putting unfair pressure on him and sometimes limiting him.

4. *Processing and sensory differences.* The typical person with Asperger Syndrome may experience the world in an unusual way in terms both of sensory input and the way he processes information.

5. *Mind blindness.* We're all mind readers, whether we realise it or not, in the sense that we have at least some natural and innate ability to 'read' nonverbal communication. Aspies are not totally 'blind' in this respect, but reading nonverbal communication is not an innate skill for them. That makes it hard for them to understand, predict and relate to other people.

6. *Rigidity.* People with AS find it genuinely hard to be flexible. This can explain some of the more baffling and maddening aspects of AS where an individual may seem to be stubborn, dogmatic, unreasonable or controlling.

7. *Social vulnerability.* This is an obvious one of course, but very worth keeping in mind.

18 Become a student

These days it is possible to find courses about Asperger Syndrome run by local autism organisations as well as colleges and universities. Of course when you are a busy parent, you may not be able to find time for study, but if your circumstances allow it, it can be worth considering.

Not every single thing you learn will apply to your child, of course, but you will probably get helpful insights which will probably help you see some of his traits in a more positive light and understand them. For example, you might see his blunt and direct approach to life as something rare and refreshing, and appreciate his lack of hypocrisy or pretence.

3

The Seven Key Insights

Key Insight # 1: Asperger extremes
Key Insight # 2: Fish out of water
Key Insight # 3: Rates of development
Key Insight # 4: Processing and sensory differences
Key Insight # 5: Mind blindness
Key Insight # 6: Rigidity
Key Insight # 7: Social vulnerability

This chapter explores Seven Key Insights which can help us to understand Asperger Syndrome:

1. Asperger extremes (page 34)

2. Fish out of water (page 38)

3. Rates of development (page 44)

4. Processing and sensory differences (page 49)

5. Mind blindness (page 55)

6. Rigidity (page 60)

7. Social vulnerability (page 65)

KEY INSIGHT # 1: ASPERGER EXTREMES

TIP BOX

Key Insight # 1: Asperger extremes

19   Understand that he's 'like anyone else, only more so'

20   Recognise extremes and opposites: His individual profile

21   Adjust your expectations

22   Extremes can offer great learning opportunities

23   Direct his strengths

19 Understand that he's 'like anyone else, only more so'

When my son, Kenneth, was small I worried about him a lot and I found him almost impossible to manage. On top of that, I found it very hard to get across to anyone the extent of my concerns. Even when I talked to friends or family, I felt like no one really 'got it'. Looking back I can understand why. First, there was a lot less awareness about Asperger Syndrome back then. I had never heard of the condition before Kenneth was diagnosed, and up till then nobody had even suggested it as a possibility. And, second, none of the difficulties I was describing really seemed that remarkable or unusual.

I didn't want to give anyone the impression that I couldn't cope, so I tried not to reveal too much to anyone. But sometimes I tried discussing my worries about Kenneth with other parents, hoping to compare notes and try to get things in proportion. But I rarely felt that they understood, and no matter what difficulty I mentioned, eating, sleeping, behaviour, socialising or whatever, I saw that they didn't really relate to it.

Sometimes they would tell me that their children had similar difficulties, and that children normally 'grow out' of these things. They probably thought I was making a fuss over nothing and I suppose the kind of responses they gave me were meant to be reassuring:

> 'Oh, my child doesn't sleep well either.'

> 'My child is a fussy eater.'

> 'Yes, I know what you mean. My child finds it hard to mix with other children. It's just a phase; he will grow out of it.'

But, far from being reassured, I was left feeling inadequate and confused, just as many parents are at times when it comes to their child's Asperger Syndrome. For it is a very complex condition; and it was only years later that I started to make sense of it. And here's the truth: Asperger Syndrome is not some alien condition. Just about every trait of AS is something that each one of us can identify with to some extent. The difference between Asperger Syndrome and so called 'normality' is often one of degree.

So if you are looking for a very simple way to get a handle on AS or explain it to other people, you just need to keep this in mind:

> *People with AS are like anyone else, only more so.*

20 Recognise extremes and opposites:
His individual profile

To make matters even more confusing, the Asperger Syndrome includes some completely opposite extremes in terms of personality, ability, etc. To take a few examples, some people with Asperger Syndrome come across as arrogant and full of themselves, while others come across as self-effacing and shy. Some are gifted at mathematics, while others have a problem understanding basic mathematical concepts. Some have a sense of humour that is keen and sophisticated, while others find it hard to recognise humour or see the point of it. Some make extreme efforts to fit in and are well behaved and easy to manage. Others reject conventional expectations from an early age and are almost impossible to manage.

As a result there is a lot of confusion about AS and there are many misconceptions. And in reality it often gets a bad press because the more sensational, troublesome extremes inevitably get more attention, while the less troublesome are more likely to go unnoticed.

Keep in mind – your child will have his or her own unique profile which may comprise a wide and complex range of extremes.

21 Adjust your expectations

Your child, like most people with AS, may be extremely able and advanced in certain academic areas and the opposite in others. This can be confusing and lead to unfair and misleading expectations. When he is younger it is hard to know which of his difficulties are within the 'normal' range so that he is likely to grow out of them. But by the time he has reached adolescence you should have a clearer idea of where his strengths and weaknesses lie.

It is only fair to let go of unrealistic expectations about him and to take off any unfair pressure to achieve. He does not want to let himself or other people down, and unrealistic expectations can set him up for failure and disappointment. But it is not a good idea to go too far in the other direction either and set the bar too low. Try to make your expectations as realistic as possible, taking into account the reality of his individual profile. Give him something to aim for that is achievable and rewarding (see also Tips 173, 175 and 280–6).

22 Extremes can offer great learning opportunities

People with AS offer us an opportunity to see some extreme examples of certain aspects of human nature – and extreme examples can be very useful learning devices. In that sense exploring AS can help us learn more about aspects of ourselves and other people. See yourself as a student not only of AS but of yourself and of human nature in general.

23 Direct his strengths

Encourage your child to be aware of where his interests and strengths lie, and guide him in the direction of a career or path in life which plays to his strengths and makes the most of them.

KEY INSIGHT # 2: FISH OUT OF WATER

TIP BOX

Key Insight # 2: Fish out of water

24   Be aware of a common thread
25   Look within: Understand being a fish out of water
26   Encourage relationships that are likely to work
27   Identify people with common interests
28   Find like minds online
29   Rejoice in Asperger originality and differences
30   Listen with sensitivity
31   Find the right moment for listening
32   Don't minimise his feelings
33   Give him some perspective
34   Share and confide

24 Be aware of a common thread

Asperger Syndrome covers a wide spectrum of people, but there is one thing which they all seem to have in common. They generally report feeling different to other people and find it hard to fit in (Lane 2004). This feeling of alienation can become more pronounced at adolescence, when they often find it hard to relate to or fit in with a peer group in the usual way, and can end up being excluded or marginalised.

25 Look within: Understand being a fish out of water

If you think back, you will probably be able to remember some point in your own life when you had that feeling of alienation – perhaps when you experienced some kind of loss, grief or trauma. At such a time you may have felt as if nobody could possibly understand what you were going through. If so, you will know that any experience of alienation can be painful and lonely, let alone the extreme experience which seems often to accompany Asperger Syndrome.

26 Encourage relationships that are likely to work

Because it is harder for a young person with AS to find people he can relate to among his peers, one of the best ways to help him feel less alone is by helping him to find people he can successfully relate to. For example:

- Work on your own relationship with him (see also Tips 119–40).

- Encourage and foster his relationship with Pivotal People (see also 'Parents and other pivotal people' in the Introduction).

- Facilitate connections with like minded people (see also Tips 256–64).

27 Identify people with common interests

Identify things he is interested in, or that you think he might become interested in, and look for ways in which he can share his interests. Socialising can be easier when it has a specific focus, so try to find a group of people who get together periodically to share an interest that appeals to him. You will have a good idea yourself about what is worth trying, whether it is a reading group, a music class or whatever.

28 Find like minds online

For a generation who grew up before computers became such a big part of life, the idea of online communication as a way of connecting with other people can still feel a bit like second best. But this is the era of the worldwide web, and when you think about it, the internet has a lot to offer to people with AS. Through the internet they have the opportunity to connect with like-minded people in a way that they never could have before, using Facebook, Twitter, chatrooms, forums, Instant Messenger and so on.

We need of course to take appropriate precautions to protect our children and make them aware of online dangers. The UK Safer Internet Centre (see Useful Websites) is a good source of information.

29 Rejoice in Asperger originality and differences

Never give your child the impression that you would prefer it if he were 'normal'. Respect and admire the originality and difference that is such an intrinsic part of Asperger Syndrome. The world needs people who have Asperger Syndrome. Do some research into the condition from this point of view (Grandin 2002) and talk to him about it. Rejoice in the fact that your child is different. It takes courage to be different, so be proud of him and make sure he knows it!

30 Listen with sensitivity

If your child wants to talk to you about feelings of loneliness or isolation, make sure to pay attention (see also Tips 176–85, 296–7 and 303). Show a genuine interest in what he is saying so he knows you are concerned. He matters to you, of course, but people with AS do not always recognise the obvious, so he may need you to tell him this in words, in a clear and matter-of-fact way. When the moment is right, your job first and foremost is to listen to what he is telling you and try not to interrupt.

31 Find the right moment for listening

Sometimes we are busy or in a rush, and we can't always have time for heart to heart discussions. That's just life, and he needs to understand that too. So if the moment is not right for intimate disclosures, don't worry. You don't need to drop everything. Tell him that you are interested in what he is telling you. It matters to you and you would love to hear more, but for whatever reason you would prefer to talk at a different time when you can listen properly.

Ideally set a time and place for a follow up – perhaps a chat over a cup of coffee or a walk together. Let him see that you are taking the arrangement seriously. Put it in your diary and suggest he does the same – and do your best not to let him down (see also Tips 130 and 137).

32 Don't minimise his feelings

We hate to think of our children feeling lonely and alienated, so it can be tempting to minimise what they are saying and try to brush it under the carpet. It's better not to do that. His reality is his reality, and it deserves to be respected. Clichés and trite solutions such as 'Don't worry' and 'It's not that bad' will not help.

Accept the reality of how he feels in a matter-of-fact way. Tell him you want to make sure you have heard and properly understood what he has told you, and you would like to say it back to him in your own words so he can tell you whether you have got it right.

Let him know you are concerned but don't overdo it by giving him the impression that you are worried sick (see also Tips 86–7 and 91–4).

33 Give him some perspective

When you are feeling bad or lonely, it can be reassuring to know that there are other people who feel the same, and that there is hope for the future.

Tell him that what he is feeling is common among people with AS. Perhaps you and he can discuss why this might be. Is it because Aspies are such unusual people and find it hard to find people who are similar to themselves?

Discuss what makes him unusual and how he might be able to find other people who are similar to him. Does he have a special interest? Perhaps he can find another person or even a group of other people who share his enthusiasm – whether it is for music, model planes, foreign language or whatever. These days people with AS have more opportunity to make contact with people online who share their interests and views on life. They can get great solace from online relationships with people who are 'on their wavelength'. It is always wise to be cautious about the internet and to ensure that your child knows how to stay safe online (see UK Safer Internet Centre in the Useful Websites section; see also Tips 256–64).

Speak to him also from the point of view of someone who is older and has more experience of life. Remind him that most people feel things very acutely at his age for various reasons, including the natural physical changes that he is going through. Reassure him that it will not always be that way. Feelings wax and wane, and he will not always feel so bad. Perhaps suggest that he does some research himself on the feelings of alienation that often go with Asperger Syndrome – the Wrong Planet website (see Useful Websites) may be a good starting point.

34 Share and confide

There may have been times in your life when you felt similar feelings to what he is feeling now, especially when you were around his age. And you must have your own stories. Don't make your story more important than his of course, but be prepared to confide in him about your own experiences of alienation, when the moment is right. This can help build the relationship between you, help him understand you better – and let him see that other people have their stories too. Invite his comments and opinions – you might be surprised by what he has to say.

KEY INSIGHT # 3: RATES OF DEVELOPMENT

TIP BOX

Key Insight # 3: Rates of development

35   Set normal milestones to the side
36   Look within: Understand rates of development
37   Comparisons are odious!
38   Beware of jumping to conclusions
39   Take a long view
40   Help him get a positive, realistic self-concept
41   Model late development in self
42   Validate and acknowledge progress
43   There's always another boat!

35 Set normal milestones to the side

Asperger Syndrome is, among other things, a developmental disorder. But it's important to be clear about what that means and what it doesn't mean.

It means that people with AS usually develop in ways that are untypical, but it *doesn't* mean they are slow developers. It's not as simple as that, because at any given stage a person with Asperger Syndrome may be unusually behind in one area of development and unusually advanced in another. In a typical picture, for example, a child may be precocious in mathematical subjects but several years behind in emotional and social development, and during adolescence he may be very out of step with his peers when it comes to social and emotional development.

36 Look within: Understand rates of development

Life can be so much easier when you don't stick out! Try to remember a time in your own life when you felt out of step with your peers in some way. For example, if as a child you were either very tall or very short for your age you may remember feeling awkward and embarrassed. Or perhaps when you were his age your friends all seemed to reach puberty before you did.

If you can remember times like these, it can give you at least some insight into what your child might be feeling.

37 Comparisons are odious!

It can be tempting to compare our children to each other or to other people's children while they are growing up, but comparisons can cause a lot of problems, so we need to be very careful.

Whenever a child feels that he is being less favourably compared to someone else, it can knock his confidence and self-esteem. But there is also a problem whenever a child feels he is being more favourably compared, because although he may enjoy a certain feeling of superiority in the moment, it can end up giving him the wrong message in the long run. In this regard, a lot depends on their confidence level, because it is not unusual for Aspies to be at one extreme or the other when it comes to confidence (or apparent confidence at any rate, for appearances can sometimes be deceptive in this regard!).

So if your child is inclined to lack confidence, comparisons can lead him to feel he needs to be better than other people in order to be good enough. If on the other hand, he is inclined to be very confident, comparison can lead him to become arrogant or even deluded.

Try your best to accept your child for who he is. And, if you can't help making comparisons, try at least to keep them to yourself.

38 Beware of jumping to conclusions

When a child develops in an untypical way, people can easily make incorrect assumptions about his ability levels and potentials. This can work in a couple of ways: if he is obviously slow in some area, there is a danger of him being written off as generally stupid. On the other hand, if he is obviously advanced in some area, it can be wrongly assumed that he is very generally clever and capable, and unfair pressure may be put on him across the board. As a result he may miss out on help that he needs in some of the other areas where he has genuine difficulty. Either way, he can end up with an unrealistic and confused self-image.

39 Take a long view

With the right attitude and learning opportunity, a person with AS is very capable of learning whatever he sets his mind to. His learning does not have to stop when he leaves school and becomes an adult. Learning should be seen as life-long. Think of the story of the tortoise and the hare. Your child can make steady progress, even in difficult areas such as social skills. There is no rush. Just think of him as (at least in some respects!) a late developer.

40 Help him get a positive, realistic self-concept

When your child's rate of development is very out of step, the world often gives him mixed and misleading messages – he can end up thinking he is a genius one day and an idiot the next! Our goal is to help him have a positive yet realistic self-concept and an accurate picture of his own strengths and weaknesses. Help him understand that it is perfectly feasible to develop at different rates in different areas and that this does not make him stupid.

41 Model late development in self

Our children learn a lot from watching how we lead our lives. If we have a positive, flexible attitude to life and learning, we can give them a concrete example of late development. For example, learning a new skill or language when you are in your 40s or 50s can be good for you and a fun challenge. But there is an added benefit. It can model for our children a flexible attitude to learning and help them see that it is never too late to learn, and that it is not always necessary to learn things at a conventional rate or stage of life.

42 Validate and acknowledge progress

Be vigilant for signs and evidence of progress from your child and make sure to acknowledge them in words.

43 There's always another boat!

Conventional education systems are generally designed with the majority in mind and, at least up till university level, they do not particularly suit people with AS, with their unusual development profiles. So it is common for people with AS to underachieve at school. But nowadays underachievement at school age does not have to affect the rest of life because there is generally a lot more flexibility in education than there used to be.

It used to be the case that if you didn't achieve the required qualifications via the conventional routes and at the conventional times, you might well have missed your chance. Your career would be more or less set on the basis of how you performed at school, and it was hard to learn and train in later life. But these days it is much more common for people to study and take up new pursuits in adulthood. There are all sorts of opportunities for adult learning: full time, part time and online. Institutions such as the Open University, for example, are well structured to suit a person with AS, and many such institutions offer a good level of support.

So if the worst comes to the worst and your child misses the boat at school age, don't worry too much. All is not lost. There is a good chance that when the time is right another boat will come along!

KEY INSIGHT # 4: PROCESSING AND SENSORY DIFFERENCES

TIP BOX

Key Insight # 4: Processing and sensory differences

44   Understand experiencing the world differently
45   Look within: Understand processing and sensory experiences
46   Don't jump to conclusions
47   Respect his need for solitude
48   Communicate clearly
49   Accept his preferred learning style
50   Avoid TMI (too much information)!
51   Suggest scripts like 'Let me think'
52   Try one to one

44 Understand experiencing the world differently

The typical person with Asperger Syndrome experiences the world in an unusual way in terms of sensory input and how he processes information. He may have his own very individual style and rate of learning. When we understand these differences it can take a lot of pressure off all round, because we can be more realistic and fair and make allowances where appropriate. We are also in a better position to help relevant other people in his life to understand and, most importantly, we can help him to understand himself.

Key differences are in the areas of:

- sensory input (unusual sensory experience, hypo or hyper sensitivity)

- nonverbal communication (difficulty tuning in to or understanding nonverbal communication)

- processing speed (processing some information unusually slowly and some unusually quickly)

- focus and attention (difficulties retaining focus in some situations yet capable of a kind of hyper-focus in others, for example in areas of special interest)

- processing overload (difficulties dealing with too much extraneous information)

- executive function (poor organisation skills and difficulties in seeing a task or project through from beginning to end)

- memory (idiosyncratic memory, sometimes very good in certain areas and poor in others)

- learning style (definite preferences for particular learning style, probably learning much better if a visual approach is used).

45 Look within: Understand processing and sensory experiences

As always it can be helpful to look within to try to gain some understanding of these differences, for in reality no two people in the world are exactly the same in how they experience the world and process information. We may find that we can relate to some typical Asperger differences, because we have probably experienced them ourselves, albeit in a much less extreme way. To take a few examples:

- Perhaps you have strong food preferences. You may absolutely hate certain foods and find them disgusting. (Sensory input)

- You may have found yourself at sea from time to time in a social situation. Perhaps you can think of a social occasion where you did not know anyone in the company and everyone else seemed to know each other, so you felt uncomfortable and out of place. (Nonverbal communication)

- We all have had times when we have been trying to learn something new and found it hard to keep up. So we know this can be a frustrating and humiliating experience. (Processing speed)

- It is not always easy to pay attention for long periods, but all of us find it easier to pay attention to something we are very interested in. (Focus and attention)

- We all know the infuriating feeling when someone is explaining something to us and they give us far too much information at once so that we cannot think straight. (Processing overload)

- Part of the reason for the popularity of life coaching is that we all need help from time to time to work our plans through to completion and convert our dreams into reality. (Executive function)

- Nobody has a perfect memory and everybody's memory is selective to some degree. (Memory)

- Most people have a way of learning that works best for them. (Learning style)

46 Don't jump to conclusions

A person with AS may process some things unusually slowly and some unusually quickly, and this can be misleading and confusing. For example, a person who is exceptionally quick at processing computer programming language may at the same time be very slow at processing mundane conversation or small talk.

This kind of disparity can be misleading, because he may seem more or less capable than he is. For example, if you meet him socially and he seems to be struggling with basic social skills such as small talk and conversation, there is a danger that you might write him off as slow or stupid. If, however, you have no experience of him socially and are only aware of his exceptional computer skills, you might expect too much from him socially because you are not aware of his processing difficulties. Don't make too many assumptions based on processing speed.

47 Respect his need for solitude

The world can be a tiring, uncomfortable place when you are dealing with processing and sensory differences constantly, and this can take its toll. Knowing this can help you understand why a young person with AS sometimes needs space and solitude. It can have a calming effect and help him think more clearly. Ideally his home and, in particular, his own room, should be his sanctuary and refuge.

48 Communicate clearly

Make it your goal to take into consideration your child's processing and sensory differences so you can communicate with him clearly and effectively.

49 Accept his preferred learning style

Everyone has a preferred learning style. Some students, coming up to an exam, will revise more successfully when they read and use key cards, because they are naturally visual learners. Others will prefer to listen to tapes because they are naturally auditory learners. And some will do best using a mixture of the two approaches. But for most people these are fairly moderate preferences and they can manage either way without too many problems.

Learning style preferences among people with AS on the other hand can be very extreme, to the point that they may have a real problem if information is presented to them in the 'wrong way'.

In practice, your child is more likely to have a strong tendency towards visual learning, but if he happens to be an auditory learner that is likely to be an extreme preference too. Encourage him to think about and figure out his own preferred learning style, and where possible make sure his educators are aware of this so they also can take it into consideration.

50 Avoid TMI (too much information)!

Don't overload him with extra information, especially when he seems to be already confused. If you are communicating with him and you feel his attention wandering, pull back. Give him a bit of time to process what you have already said. Or perhaps try summarising what you have said in a clear, simple way and ask him to repeat it back to you. This can help clarify it in his mind and let you know he has understood.

51 Suggest scripts like 'Let me think'

Suggest to him a few scripts he can fall back on in situations where he needs time to think or process information. For example:

> 'Let me think.'

> 'Give me a moment to think about that.'

> 'I will need a few days to think that through, then we can discuss it again.'

52 Try one to one

In general one-to-one communication is much easier for Aspies – fewer people mean fewer sensory and processing complications!

KEY INSIGHT # 5: MIND BLINDNESS

TIP BOX

Key Insight # 5: Mind blindness

53   Understand mind reading
54   Look within: Understand mind blindness
55   Don't confuse mind blindness with immorality
56   Empathy works both ways
57   Translate the subtext
58   Explain the social rules
59   Nonverbal communication is hard to learn
60   Spell out 'the obvious'
61   Encourage him to find ways to please
62   Be patient
63   Be aware of him feeling 'peopled out'
64   Build up gradually from one to one

53 Understand mind reading

Most people can 'read minds' in the sense that they are able to understand the nonverbal communication which is such an important part of social communication. Nonverbal communication serves many purposes but in general it has the function of helping things run smoothly between people. Body language for example lets us imagine what other people are probably thinking, expecting or intending, without them having to tell us in words, and we naturally take this information into account in deciding how to respond. Mind reading is a complex skill, but we do it all the time without thinking about it. To take a simple example, when we figure out that someone is angry solely from their manner and tone of voice, we are in a sense reading that person's mind rather than literally hearing his words.

Some people are naturally better at nonverbal communication than others, but people with AS are sometimes referred to as being 'mind blind' because they have real difficulties with nonverbal communication. Mind blindness is a major cause of the communication problems which can put Aspies at such a disadvantage in life and can make them so vulnerable socially, especially at this age.

Mind blindness is a very real handicap to social success, but it is a difficulty that may not be obvious to outsiders, which is one of the reasons why AS is sometimes referred to as a 'hidden disability'.

54 Look within: Understand mind blindness

Think of a time when you may have offended someone or got the wrong end of the stick when dealing with another person. At such a time for whatever reason you were 'mind blind' in the sense that you did not correctly read the state of mind of the other person.

55 Don't confuse mind blindness with immorality

Sometimes people judge Aspies harshly when they do something that seems to reveal a lack of empathy. But if your child has not been aware of the perspective of the other person, it is very difficult for him to empathise with it. We need to be absolutely clear that this is a real disability and not a lack of morality. If your child has a genuine blind spot, the fair thing to do is help fill in that blind spot, not judge him for it.

Mind blindness does not imply lack of integrity or moral fibre; in fact it is often the opposite. Once a person with AS sees the point and knows the right thing to do, he often steps up in an exceptionally courageous way.

56 Empathy works both ways

Mind blindness makes it more difficult to imagine the perspective of another person. One way to try to help your child is by drawing his attention to the point of view of another person and encouraging him to empathise. Remember, he is the one with the real disability, so it is only fair that we take responsibility for bridging the empathy gap.

57 Translate the subtext

People often do not mean what they say or say what they mean. That's just how the world works. We give compliments we don't mean. We tell white lies. We are economical with the truth. We exaggerate. But all these things do not come very easily or naturally to Aspies which can leave them vulnerable. Adolescent girls for example can be sexually naive and misread the intentions of males who give them attention. We can help in such situations by translating the subtext – in other words the unspoken truth of what is going on and what people probably have in mind.

58 Explain the social rules

An Aspie doesn't have a very reliable social antenna. This makes him inclined to get it wrong a lot of the time and break rules he doesn't even know exist. And the world makes him pay, especially at this age. Try to explain the social rules to him in a clear logical way (see Tips 224–40).

59 Nonverbal communication is hard to learn

Up to a point you can teach your child to mind read and he can improve at nonverbal communication, but it will never be easy or natural. In order to learn and understand nonverbal communication he probably needs to consciously engage his intellect rather than rely on his intuition, as most people do, and that can be hard work.

60 Spell out 'the obvious'

It is easy to wrongly assume that your child should know certain things intuitively. But 'the obvious' is not always obvious to someone with Asperger Syndrome so you may need to spell out clearly what people may want or expect, and what the impact of his choices and behaviour might be. To take a simple example, it may not occur to him that if he rarely answers his phone or replies to texts, people may assume that he doesn't want to bother with them or become so frustrated that they eventually stop trying to contact him.

61 Encourage him to find ways to please

Aspies can appear selfish when they don't do the small things that please people – enquiring about someone's health, making small talk, offering a cup of tea, buying a present, etc. But sometimes they simply do not think of these things. So it is sometimes worth pointing out to your child how he could make someone else happy by means of a small gesture. Just tell him in a simple, matter-of-fact way without giving him a guilt trip, 'I imagine X will be really happy if...'

62 Be patient

In order to help your child, part of your job is to teach him the Social Curriculum (see Tips 224–40) which involves explaining nonverbal communication, spelling things out and filling in a lot of blanks. But nonverbal communication is like a foreign language to him. And it is far more complex than most languages. He may forget what you told him and get it wrong time and again – so you may need to tell him the same thing time and again. Be prepared – you are going to need a lot of patience!

63 Be aware of him feeling 'peopled out'

Don't forget that the business of trying to figure people out can be exhausting for a person with AS and when he has to deal with people for too long he can end up becoming 'peopled out'.

64 Build up gradually from one to one

Sometimes he may lose confidence socially and retreat. And that may be OK for a while if it is what he needs. But at some point you may need to entice him back in to the world and encourage him to engage. Keep in mind that he may be much more comfortable relating to people in a one-to-one setting, and that you may need to build up from that gradually.

KEY INSIGHT # 6: RIGIDITY

TIP BOX

Key Insight # 6: Rigidity

65   Rigidity explains a lot!

66   Know that stubborn is a stubborn word

67   Consider trains versus cars

68   Look within: Understand rigidity in yourself

69   Be aware that change can be difficult

70   Don't mislead

71   Nobody can be good at everything

72   Encourage a healthy attitude to mistakes

73   Use some verbal tricks

65 Rigidity explains a lot!

A tendency to be rigid is at the core of Asperger Syndrome. It manifests in many ways and can help explain many aspects of AS that are hard to understand otherwise. For example:

- resistance to change
- dislike of uncertainty
- the craving for order, routine and predictability
- the tendency to be obsessive
- wanting to be right
- difficulty making decisions
- perfectionism
- resistance to correction and criticism.

66 Know that stubborn is a stubborn word

'Rigid' can be a good and insightful adjective – better than other adjectives like 'stubborn' which are often used to describe various manifestations of AS that people find annoying, frustrating and unreasonable.

As well as apparent stubbornness, Asperger rigidity can help to explain behaviour and attitudes which come across as:

- wilful
- dogmatic
- overbearing
- controlling
- dominant
- obsessive
- ritualistic
- extremely routine-based
- unreasonable
- hard to work with.

67 Consider trains versus cars

The train track analogy can be a good way to understand Asperger rigidity. Think about the difference between trains and cars. Most people's brains are more like cars, in the sense that they can drive along the road in a particular direction, but if they like they can also quite easily take a turn, change direction, pull in to the side of the road or stop. The Asperger brain, on the other hand, is more like a train on a train track. When it sets off in a particular direction it keeps going towards its destination in a very fixed and rigid way, and it is much harder for it to slow down, stop or change direction.

68 Look within: Understand rigidity in yourself

We can all be rigid at times of course so we know to a certain extent what it is like. We enjoy our favourite routines and rituals, and there are times when the most important thing to us is our need to be right.

If you think about your own rigidity you might notice that whenever you are anxious or under stress you often find it harder than usual to be flexible. And we know that anxiety is commonly associated with Asperger Syndrome. So this can give you some insight into your child's perspective and help you realise that sometimes he genuinely does find it difficult to be flexible.

69 Be aware that change can be difficult

Most people find change stressful to some degree, but for people with AS it can be extremely stressful. That in itself makes adolescence difficult for your child because it is a time of great change, when life can suddenly seem very unpredictable.

Keep in mind the huge number of changes that your child goes through during this period and make appropriate allowances. He has to cope with all the usual changes such as physical and hormonal changes, as well as changing expectations socially and academically. All this can be overwhelming for the young person with AS, and make his journey through adolescence exceptionally stressful. He may experience extreme teenage angst and mood swings, and often without much compensation by way of a peer group network.

70 Don't mislead

Do your bit to make life predictable for him by encouraging a healthy level of order and structure, explaining things and communicating clearly (see Tips 205–16).

Be honest with him about expectations and don't make false promises.

71 Nobody can be good at everything

Counter paralysing perfectionism by reminding him that no one is good at everything, and by confiding in him about your own shortcomings.

72 Encourage a healthy attitude to mistakes

Help him to see that making mistakes is inevitable. The best attitude to mistakes involves facing and accepting them, then figuring out what is to be learned from them and what he might do differently next time.

73 Use some verbal tricks

Aspies can be very skilful with words. Sometimes you can end up tied up in knots when you are trying to reason with him, or discuss something, and especially when you are trying to tell him something he doesn't want to hear. When he is being argumentative and unreasonable try some of the following:

- *Plant seeds.* When he is rigidly sticking to some obviously unreasonable point of view, sometimes there is no point in trying to offer an alternative view. Think of yourself as planting seeds instead. Insert a remark into the conversation and then leave it at that. If he rejects your remark or idea, give the impression that it is no big deal to you and don't try to force the issue. Let it go for the moment. You have planted the seed of an idea in his head, and it is possible that he will think it over when the time is right.

- *Polar extremes.* If you and he get into an entrenched argument, where he is taking one extreme point of view and you are taking the other, try the game of polar extremes, whereby you swap positions and each take the point of view of the other! Obviously this needs to be done in the spirit of goodwill and not taken too seriously, but it can be an interesting exercise if the mood and moment is right.

  You need to explain to him the point of the exercise – it is an exercise in imagination and it might help each of you to see the point of view of the other. The aim of the game is to enter into the other's mindset as fully and convincingly as possible. You can make it fun by swapping seats and giving each other marks for skills of persuasiveness.

- *PMI (plus, minus, interesting).* Choices and decisions can be tortuous when you have AS. Encourage him to make a PMI – a list of what he sees as the plus factors, the minus factors and the interesting ones, and then weigh the situation up.

KEY INSIGHT # 7: SOCIAL VULNERABILITY

TIP BOX

Key Insight # 7: Social vulnerability

74   Don't expect other people to get it

75   Recognise that it's a hidden disability

76   Social punishments can be very real

77   Keep an eye on the company he keeps

78   Make sure he is aware of danger

79   Be vigilant

80   Be prepared in case bullying occurs

81   Help him learn the Social Curriculum

82   Don't take things personally

83   Never leave him friendless

84   Appreciate the value of friends and family

85   Don't let him get 'peopled out'

See also Tip 47, Respect his need for solitude.

74 Don't expect other people to get it

Young people with AS are often more vulnerable than they appear. But because to outsiders they generally seem fairly 'normal' we cannot expect other people to really understand. That makes it all the more important that at least we, as their parents, do our best to understand.

75 Recognise that it's a hidden disability

Social difficulties are a normal part of AS. They can make life difficult and complicated, especially at this age. In order to help and make appropriate allowances, we first need to get to grips with the reality of social difficulties and the extent of their impact.

For example:

- Social maturity, understanding and reasoning may be delayed by an average three years (Attwood 2006b) leaving your child at sea in the complex and rapidly changing social world of his peers during adolescence.

- Social awkwardness and lack of confidence can affect his academic performance.

- It may be hard for him to do himself justice in interview situations.

- Difficulty in reading the intentions of others can leave him vulnerable. He may be ill equipped to judge people and make good choices about who to associate with.

- He may have a problem relating to people in authority. At one extreme he may treat teachers and other people in authority without appropriate respect or deference, because he is either oblivious of the concept of authority or rebellious. At the other extreme he may be overly apprehensive of people in authority. Either extreme can make it difficult for him to relate in a balanced, productive way to people in authority in his life who might otherwise be able to help him.

- To compensate for social problems, some young people with AS learn to get attention by engaging in outrageous behaviour. He may act up and get a reputation for being the school clown. When he becomes notorious in this way the young person with AS may misinterpret the attention as popularity and wrongly believe that the people who are laughing at him and setting him up are his genuine friends.

This can lead him to get into bad company, perhaps with a peer group who are involved in wild, excessive behaviour, and who tolerate the kid with AS for a bit of a 'laugh' and set him up.

For young Aspie girls, this kind of naivety and poor judgement can lead them to engage in foolish and irresponsible sexual behaviour and even promiscuity.

76 Social punishments can be very real

This is the sad truth that we need to be aware of. Social 'punishments' include isolation, judgement, ridicule, humiliation and bullying. And punishments like this can take their toll. They can adversely affect levels of confidence, self-esteem, academic progress and so on, and ultimately lead to depression.

77 Keep an eye on the company he keeps

Without appearing too intrusive, keep a discreet eye on who your child is spending time with. Ideally, if you know his friends' parents, make contact with them and keep channels of communication open.

78 Make sure he is aware of danger

Aim to make sure he knows about any dangers he needs to be aware of, especially at his age – dangers, for example, associated with alcohol, drugs, sex and 'bad company'.

Talk to him in a matter-of-fact way without unduly frightening him or making him paranoid. Explain calmly, clearly and logically that you are concerned about certain things and tell him why: that you love him and don't want to see him getting into a bad situation or doing something that might adversely affect his life for a long time to come. Be specific and talk about exactly what the dangers are.

It is probably better to look at and quote facts and statistics rather than come across as hysterical or controlling. In fact, if you can persuade him to research relevant statistics for himself and report back to you, that may be even better.

79 Be vigilant

Young people with AS tend to attract two very different groups of people – the maternal and the predatory (Attwood 2006a, 2013). Keep an eye on the company your child is keeping with this in mind. Without worrying too much or becoming paranoid, be vigilant for signs of bullying or depression (see also Tips 80 and 287–303).

80 Be prepared in case bullying occurs

Because your child is at higher than normal risk of bullying, it is a good idea to think ahead and have a strategy prepared just in case. For example:

- To minimise the risk of bullying, try to avoid situations where your child is left without whatever protection you think he needs. Aim, for example, to have a trusted friend with him in situations where he might be vulnerable to 'predators'.

- Be vigilant for signs of bullying. Young people sometimes do not like to admit they are being bullied, but keep an eye out for telltale signs such as money missing, cuts, bruises, sleeping problems, depression, etc.

- Listen and take him seriously if he confides in you about bullying. Tell him he has done the right thing to confide in you, that you are completely on his side and want to do all you can to help.

- Establish the facts as objectively as you can. It is always possible that he is getting the wrong end of the stick or getting things out of proportion. If he is, try to help him make better sense of the situation and see it more realistically. But, if it seems to be a case of genuine bullying, tell him that he does not deserve to be treated in this way and that you will do all you can to help.

- Liaise with your child to keep accurate records of all incidents of bullying, with dates and details.

- Report all cases of bullying to the appropriate authorities and encourage the young person to do the same.

- Seek medical help for physical bullying or in respect of any psychological impact.

81 Help him learn the Social Curriculum

There is a certain amount we can to do help him learn social skills. We can do this in various ways but by far the most valuable way is by means of our own relationship with him (see also Tips 130–40).

82 Don't take things personally

It is understandable that outsiders often take offence at typical AS ways of relating, for they can at times come across as gauche, offhand, unfriendly, rude, dismissive, pedantic, boring or patronising. I remember once, for example, a teacher taking offence after a disagreement with my son, when he told her he 'would like to see her at lunch time'. In a way there was nothing intrinsically wrong with what he said, so in his mind it was perfectly reasonable. He had no idea that he had come across as defiant and cheeky. Or that it was an inappropriate thing for a student to say to the teacher and in the circumstances it would normally have been the other way round!

It is very tempting for us as parents to take offence too at some of the things our children say and do, but we should try our best not to take things personally, and realise that usually no offence is intended.

83 Never leave him friendless

Encourage and nurture relationships that you know are good for him, for example with the pivotal people in his life. Consider enlisting the help of a befriender (National Autistic Society 2013a). And of course nurture your own relationship with your child, so he knows that if all else fails at least he always has you.

84 Appreciate the value of friends and family

Blood is thicker than water and family members can be great allies over the long term. Encourage your family to support each other and in particular your child with AS. Help them understand Asperger Syndrome as well. Do what you can to help siblings and other family members to understand each other's perspectives and difficulties, and to view each other generously.

85 Don't let him get 'peopled out'

Accept the reality that simply being with other people can sometimes be very tiring for Aspies. It is natural to be anxious about a young person who seems to be withdrawing from the world too much. And it's good to entice and encourage him into the world. But we need to aim for a balance and not force too much.

I got a good insight into this one day when I was talking to a young Aspie who was doing his best to hold down a job. It was a job that suited him. He loved it and his employers were delighted with him, but he was feeling the strain in a very big way. It was not laziness. It was exhaustion from having to deal with people.

'I'm not sure if I can go on much longer,' he told me. 'I feel like I'm getting burnt out.'

It seemed like a real shame to me and I was keen to understand.

'What do you think has got you feeling this way?' I asked him.

His answer was a real eye opener: 'I think I'm just peopled out,' he said.

(See also Tip 47, Respect his need for solitude.)

4

The Best Approach

Being calm and assertive
Parenting with confidence
Being pragmatic
Encouraging motivation
Avoiding conflict

The ideal parenting approach for a young person with Asperger Syndrome – or any young person for that matter – is one that involves:

- Being calm and assertive (page 74)

- Parenting with confidence (page 76)

- Being pragmatic (page 80)

- Encouraging motivation (page 85)

- Avoiding conflict (page 88)

All that makes sense in theory, but it is not always easy in practice. This chapter contains some ideas that might help you pull it off.

BEING CALM AND ASSERTIVE

TIP BOX

Being calm and assertive

86 Recognise the value of a calm and assertive approach

87 Be relaxed

88 Explain consequences calmly

89 Use fewer words

90 When you lose your temper you have lost

86 Recognise the value of a calm and assertive approach

Being calm and assertive is a powerful position to adopt. When you are calm and assertive you are in a better position to handle whatever comes along. You help your child feel more secure, and hopefully he will learn from your example to approach life in a calmer, more assertive way too.

87 Be relaxed

Make it a goal to be relaxed. And even if it is not in your basic nature, do what you can to learn to relax – meditate, pray, practise yoga, read a book, book a massage. Do whatever works for you, but make relaxation a priority. If you have a birthday coming up and people are wondering what you might like as a present, why not ask for some kind of gift to help you relax – perhaps tickets for an evening out, a spa voucher or even an agreement to babysit to allow you some time off.

88 Explain consequences calmly

At this age it is very natural for young people to test the boundaries. When this happens, decide at the outset whether this battle is really worth pursuing right now. If it is, figure out what consequences, positive or negative, should follow your child's choices and behaviour and make the consequences fair, realistic, proportionate and as easy to enforce as possible. Aim to explain and deliver the consequences as calmly and decisively as you can. If it is not, consider turning a blind eye, at least for the moment.

89 Use fewer words

Try not to get drawn into prolonged controversy. When you put a lot of effort into trying to convince and persuade your child about something, either to force him to see things a particular way or to adopt a particular course of action, this can come across as weakness and make him less secure. Unless the issue really warrants it, be prepared to let go of the outcome for now. Fewer words can be more powerful than many in some circumstances. And don't worry too much about having the *last* word in an argument. It is more important to have the *lasting* word!

90 When you lose your temper you have lost

We all lose our cool sometimes. That's life. The best we can do is to try to minimise times like that and try to remember in the heat of the moment that shouting, yelling and threatening rarely solve anything. They usually just make matters worse and give a bad example (see also Tips 118, 308–10 and 318).

PARENTING WITH CONFIDENCE

TIP BOX

Parenting with confidence

91   Parent with confidence
92   Have faith in yourself
93   Fake it till you make it
94   Use humour

91 Parent with confidence

Maybe it's not true to say that all young people with AS are difficult to manage, but it is probably safe to say that most are! This alone can seriously undermine your confidence in your parenting abilities. I know this from my own experience, for I have raised two children, and only one of them has AS. My daughter was mostly pretty manageable, even through her adolescent years, whereas Kenneth was generally very difficult. So by the time he reached adolescence I had come to seriously doubt my parenting abilities. Every time I found myself at a loss to understand him or know how to handle him, my confidence took a knock, and I know from talking to other parents that this kind of feeling is not unusual.

Confidence is important. It helps us function better as parents. When we exude a confident, assured air, our children feel more secure so that hopefully they are less likely to act up. But even when they do, we are in a better position to deal with the challenge, and things around us run more smoothly.

During your children's adolescence, your confidence will be tested, so find ways to build it up. For example:

- Don't compare yourself to other parents who seem to be doing a better job – and don't let other people compare you either. They are not in your situation.

- Remind yourself that you are a capable, accomplished person. You have many gifts and abilities, and you have achieved a lot of positive things in your life. If needs be, sit down and write a list – perhaps with someone else you trust who knows you well and appreciates you, and draw up the list together.

- Remind yourself that your situation is a difficult one. Your child is at a difficult age, and you are doing a good job in the circumstances. You do not need to be perfect.

- As far as possible seek out and include in your life other people who appreciate and respect you. The people we have in our life can make a big difference to how we feel about ourselves.

92 Have faith in yourself

A child or young person with AS usually has many professionals and experts involved in his life, for example doctors, psychologists, teachers and so on. And there are countless books, articles, websites, television programmes, and so on where we can learn about AS and find out the opinions of the experts. All this is very helpful but, sometimes when we turn to experts for help, this can also have the effect of undermining our confidence. For no matter how useful such help may be, the idea that someone else knows more and understands your child better than you do can be a bitter pill for a parent to swallow.

It is of course a good idea to educate yourself about AS and learn all you can from the experts, but in reality you know your child in a way that other people could not possibly know him. So, as well as listening to the advice of others, remember to listen to your own judgement. Don't forget that as a parent you are an expert too – an expert on your own child.

93 Fake it till you make it

Being confident is easier said than done, and it can take time to build (or rebuild!) confidence. So while it may not make sense to put yourself under pressure by being false, sometimes it's a good idea to 'fake it till you make it'. If you can manage to behave in an apparently confident way, this can make you feel more confident in the moment. 'Faking it till you make it' may mean various things, for example:

- Deliberately adopting a quiet, assured manner, posture, etc.

- Taking your time! In the heat of the moment it can sometimes be hard to know how to respond to people or situations that threaten our confidence. Take time to respond to people and situations in a thoughtful measured way, especially when you are feeling pressured or rushed.

- Speaking clearly and quietly.

- Sounding interested rather than opinionated.

- Keeping your tone neutral. If you find this difficult, use this simple trick. Imagine for a moment a documentary is being made about your child and you are the interviewer. Adopt the tone you imagine the interviewer might adopt – pleasant, interested and unemotional.

- Not rising to the bait when things become heated.

- Removing yourself from a heated situation, or deliberately taking the heat out of the situation by deflection, changing the subject, etc.

- Having a 'script' ready. One thing which can be helpful is to mentally prepare a simple phrase or 'script' to help you deal with situations which undermine your confidence. This may be something as simple as 'I need time to think about that', 'I don't want to discuss this at the moment', 'I am not happy with how you are behaving', 'I don't have to give you a reason' and so on. Be prepared to repeat your script parrot-fashion if necessary.

- If you are upset or irritated and you feel the need to let your child know, say so in words calmly and directly and try not to let it spill out in less direct ways – sarcasm, accusation and so on.

94 Use humour

Lighten up! There are always problems but life still goes on. Have the confidence to take life and your problems less seriously and trust that everything is going to be OK. Humour can be a very powerful tool!

BEING PRAGMATIC

TIP BOX

Being pragmatic

95   Do what works

96   Agree rather than impose

97   Know you can't deal with everything at once

98   Cultivate patience

99   Reserve your opinion

100 Go along with things

101 Understand that timing is everything

95 Do what works

When it comes to parenting there are many different ideas and approaches which you can try. How do you decide which ones are worth going with and which you should kick into touch? Have confidence in your own judgement, but remember – there is no point in all the philosophies in the world unless they work! So use this very simple rule: Only do what works – and for as long as it works!

96 Agree rather than impose

Realistically speaking, life is easier all round when your child does not feel you are trying to control him, so sometimes even when you *know* you know best, it can work better if you do not impose your ideas and solutions. This can be just a matter of timing, whereby you hold back and wait for the right moment before contributing your input to a situation, rather than jumping in when you know it will probably be seen as controversial.

If you can somehow 'manipulate' a situation or conversation in such a way that your child, rather than you, comes up with the very solution that you know is best for him, that is obviously ideal. If you can manage this, it is a pretty neat trick to pull off. There is less likelihood of arguments or rebellion and your child's self-esteem will be enhanced by a certain degree of autonomy.

As an example, imagine your child has been invited to an event and for good reasons you are uneasy about him going to it. Instead of telling him starkly that there is 'no way' he would be allowed to attend the event, try to steer the discussion so that he is more likely to take a sensible decision about it himself. Perhaps suggest that you set aside a time to discuss it, and when you do so:

- Adopt a calm and confident manner. Try not to sound too anxious about the situation.

- Use a tone of interest and enquiry (see also Tips 176–85) with phrases such as 'That sounds interesting', 'How do you feel about it?'

- Ask key questions such as 'How do you plan to get there?' What time will it end? What do you know about the venue? Is it well supervised? How has this event gone previously? Has there ever been trouble and, if so, how was it handled?

- Appeal to his logic and common sense. Suggest that he talks to someone who knows more than you or he do, because obviously it makes sense to make a decision with as much relevant information to hand as possible. (Perhaps you can then tip off the person who he will be talking to, so they can have the relevant facts and figures at their fingertips.)

- Offer to find out what you can, but say it would actually be more helpful if he did some research himself. Suggest that it would make more sense to discuss it again after he does and to leave a final decision in the meantime, because it is always more intelligent to make decisions which are as informed as possible.

When adolescents feel they are being controlled it can get their backs up and they can end up doing the very opposite of what you want them to do, purely because they want to be in charge. So hopefully the very fact that you have not come across as controlling will make a sensible way forward more likely. Of course there will always be times when you need to impose a decision on your child for his own good, but at this age it is generally better to be pragmatic and to agree decisions where you can.

97 Know you can't deal with everything at once

We feel daunted sometimes when it seems like there are too many things to deal with. But realistically speaking, you can only deal with one thing at a time. Step back and make a list of all the issues requiring your attention and rate them in terms of priority. Perhaps this is a job you can do along with a friend or family member. Figure out which of the issues you want to tackle right away and get going on them. Make a plan and timescale for issues that are less urgent, and then let the rest go, at least for the meantime.

This is a strategy that you can encourage and help your child to use which can help him deal with issues in his life when he feels daunted himself.

98 Cultivate patience

We all know how important patience is – and how difficult! But it is easier in the end if you can let go control and trust in the big picture. Life doesn't always work out on our timescale – sometimes we just need to accept it.

99 Reserve your opinion

Often as parents we know that we have good advice to offer our children, but at this age they may have little interest in what we have to say. During adolescence it is often wiser to hold back your advice. Aim to reserve your opinion and advice while nurturing your relationship with him generally, and you should find over time that there will be more and more occasions when he actually asks for your input and values it.

100 Go along with things

When you are faced with inappropriate behaviour, depending on how serious it is, of course, don't feel you always have to deal with it right away. Unless the moment is right for you to tackle a particular issue, sometimes it makes sense to go along with things and turn a blind eye – at least for the meantime.

101 Understand that timing is everything

Be sensitive about timing and choose timing that makes sense. For example:

- Remember, Aspies 'don't do spontaneity'. So give your child advance warning about what to expect, and especially about any upcoming changes.

- When introducing change, aim to minimise stress and pressure.

- You may need to allow extra processing time when your child is tired or under pressure (see also Tips 44–52).

- For important talks for example where he has something he wants to share with you, or vice versa, wait for the right moment when you can both give the talk the attention it deserves. Perhaps it warrants the right setting as well as the right time – a walk together or a meal out, or a coffee together in a coffee shop?

- If your child has had a recent diagnosis he will need time for inner adjustment, to get used to the idea and to learn about Asperger Syndrome. Don't pressurise him to talk about Asperger Syndrome or his diagnosis too much before he is ready.

(See also Tips 110 and 116 on avoiding conflict.)

ENCOURAGING MOTIVATION

TIP BOX

Encouraging motivation

102   Understand his agenda
103   Believe in him
104   Help him see the point
105   Use the project approach
106   Get him on the train
107   Offer limited reassurance
108   Find the ideal motivator

See also Tips 280–6.

102 Understand his agenda

Motivation is often an issue when it comes to Asperger Syndrome, but it can be a complex one – to say that Aspies are generally *difficult* to motivate would be too simplistic. As is often the case with AS, it is common to find two very opposite extremes at play. So while a young person with AS may seem at times to be extremely lethargic and disinterested, if he finds the right thing to be interested in things may be dramatically different. He can become interested and motivated to the point of obsession sometimes, but usually in an area or topic of his own choosing. His agenda is the one that really matters, so the trick is often to identify where his interests lie and catch the wave of where these are naturally leading him.

103 Believe in him

It is natural and understandable at this age that he wants to take the reins of his own life, and that he is not so motivated to do what his parents want him to do. This is something you may have no choice but to accept. But when it comes to bigger decisions such as college and career choices, for example, it can be hard to deal with a young person with AS who shows little interest in any of the alternatives on offer.

It is natural to worry at this stage, and it can be tempting to put energy into forcing, persuading, cajoling, pressurising and so on, in an effort to help him see the point and take an intelligent interest. But what he may really need from you at this stage is the message that you believe in him. So you might have to step back and wait till he is ready to take the reins. It may take time for him to figure out what he wants to do but, hopefully, when he does, the motivation will be coming from him, and his plans will proceed more successfully.

104 Help him see the point

Use logic and point out the obvious (see also Tips 53–64). Keep in mind that as a rule of thumb, people with AS are more likely to be motivated to become involved in things when they see the point.

105 Use the project approach

Motivation can be improved sometimes by presenting tasks in the form of challenges or projects, particularly if he is brought in to the project at an early stage and involved in the design and planning.

106 Get him on the train

Getting him to be motivated is sometimes a bit like getting him on a train. It can be hard to get him on the correct train and the timing needs to be right. But if you do, a powerful momentum can sweep things along (see also Tips 19–23).

107 Offer limited reassurance

When he believes he is doing well, that in itself can improve motivation, so don't forget about the power of praise (Matthews 2009). On the other hand, too much reassurance can seem patronising and cause resentment, so aim for balance and be careful not to over-praise.

108 Find the ideal motivator

Most of us perform better when we have an incentive or motivator, and it is no different for people with AS. External motivators, star charts and so forth can work well for young children, but more sophisticated reward schemes are more appropriate for adolescents, and they may need to work them out and come up with them for themselves. But for young people with AS the ideal motivator will be internal rather than external – the feeling that he is doing well and successfully engaged in the world (see also Tips 141–75).

AVOIDING CONFLICT

TIP BOX

Avoiding conflict

109   Model harmony
110   Choose your battles carefully
111   ACT
112   Spell it out
113   Involve him
114   Guard the line in the sand
115   Use scripts, affirmations and sound bites
116   Nip it in the bud
117   Be in it to win it
118   Recognise what not to do in the heat of the moment

109 Model harmony

Overall it is much better to avoid conflict in the first place than have to deal with it and pick up the pieces after it has arisen. It is not always possible to avoid conflict, of course, but it is at least a worthy goal. Our children may not always listen to us, but they do always watch – and they learn a lot from what they see. So try to avoid drama and uproar in the home, even when you are tired and at the end of your tether. If you can model a harmonious atmosphere in your personal life and family, conflict is bound to be less likely.

110 Choose your battles carefully

If you get into a pattern of habitual conflict with your child, both of you can end up becoming acclimatised to that status quo, to the extent that it becomes a kind of bad habit and hard to break. So unless your child is really crossing the line, it is often better to turn a blind eye.

111 ACT

It is a good idea to avoid conflict, but it is also important to know when to step in, because there will be times when conflict is needed in order to resolve a difficult situation or to defend boundaries that have been set for the benefit of yourself and your child. The acronym ACT can be useful to help you remember the basic principles whereby you:

> A – Avoid conflict (see Tips 112, 113 and 115).

> C – Choose your battles carefully (see Tips 114 and 115).

> T– Take action decisively (see Tips 116–18).

112 Spell it out

Young people with AS need to know and appreciate knowing where they stand and what the rules are; and they feel most secure when they can accurately predict the consequences of their behaviour and choices. To this end:

- Spell out to him that, while you would much prefer not to be in conflict with him, conflict may be inevitable in certain circumstances.

- Tell him that there are boundaries in life, and that you care enough about him – and yourself – to defend those boundaries. Even if it involves temporary conflict it is important, for his sake and for yours, that you do not turn a blind eye or procrastinate when certain boundaries are crossed.

- You deserve to be treated with dignity and respect – as does your child – and when someone treats you otherwise they are crossing a 'line in the sand'. Be very clear in your own mind where the line in the sand actually is.

- Make sure your child knows about the line in the sand and understands the reasoning. Be very specific and clear. Give examples of what might constitute crossing the line and if it feels right invite his input and suggestions.

- Try not to turn a blind eye when he – or anyone else for that matter – crosses your line in the sand.

- Tell him in a clear matter-of-fact way what the consequences will be when the line is crossed. Consequences should be fair and transparent.

- Discuss with him the difference between aggression and assertiveness – both aim to get you what you want, but assertiveness is more effective because it is not about antagonising people.

113 Involve him

Your child may enjoy being involved in coming up with ideas which might help you avoid conflict, for example, a written behavioural contract. If he is interested, ask him to think about goals, consequences and so on.

114 Guard the line in the sand

Avoiding conflict does not mean peace at any price. There are certain situations where you should never procrastinate or sweep things under the carpet. Always take seriously, for example, violence and abuse. Do not issue empty threats and in extreme cases step in as early as possible (see also Tips 304–25).

115 Use scripts, affirmations and sound bites

Sometimes in the heat of a challenging situation it is very hard to think clearly or to find the 'right words'. For example, perhaps your child seems to be pushing your buttons deliberately, or trying to get the upper hand. He may be persistently demanding an answer to a question, or an explanation as to why he is not allowed to do a certain thing. And at times like these, it is all too easy to say something that you regret and which may only serve to make the situation worse.

What kind of challenging situations do you think you are likely to meet, based on your experience of your own child? It can be useful to think this through and prepare in advance for such situations by coming up with some words of your own, which will hopefully allow you to think clearly and know what to say in the heat of the moment. For this purpose it can be helpful to prepare your own selection of **scripts**, **affirmations** or **sound bites**.

A **script** might be something as simple as 'I don't want to discuss this at the moment' or '*When* you have calmed down *then* we will talk about this' (notice the use of 'When...then...' as per Tip 309).

An **affirmation** generally comprises a short phrase which is formatted in a specific way and designed to foster and encourage a positive mental attitude. It is meant to be frequently repeated to oneself internally, and may help keep your thinking processes clear during times of stress.

A **sound bite** might consist of just a few short words which are easy to remember when you are under stress, and which are designed to sum up the essence of a specific helpful idea. For example, a simple, short sound bite such as 'Not now' may be enough to prevent you from speaking or acting in anger or with undue haste – simply by reminding you that people rarely make wise or rational decisions and judgements in the heat of the moment.

116 Nip it in the bud

Step in early when you notice undesirable behavioural patterns emerging. It is important to stop bad habits before they become too firmly entrenched. Sometimes that may involve challenging and drawing attention to them, but sometimes it may involve pulling away and ignoring them.

As an example, I remember my son once being rude to me and ending a phone call abruptly. I felt like ringing him back immediately to challenge him about it. But if I had done so at the time, I would have been angry and so would he, and things might well have escalated. Instead I let the dust settle, but I backed off from him for a while and avoided speaking to him on the phone until a considerable time had gone by and the atmosphere was much better between us. By that time the incident had blown over and it didn't happen again, whereas if I had tackled it more directly it might have led us along a more combative path.

So nipping things in the bud does not always mean taking action. Sometimes it just involves withholding attention.

117 Be in it to win it

It is never a good idea to get into a situation of conflict with your child, especially about a serious issue, only to end up losing. Of course you need to be fair and reasonable, but don't step into the ring, so to speak, unless you are sure of winning. 'Winning' should never be about scoring points over him, humiliating him or being mean or cruel. It is about letting him see you take control on your terms and in a masterful way.

Imagine for example, you have ended up in conflict with him about the issue of getting a tattoo (i.e. he wants to get a tattoo and you are against the idea). You have refused to back down and so has he. You have told him that you are not prepared to accept his disobedience in this, and if he insists you will remove the plug from the computer in his bedroom for a week. At this point, even if you are having second thoughts and wish you had not made such an issue about it, it is better to stick to your guns and deliver the consequence that you have threatened if he goes ahead. It will annoy and inconvenience him, but it is not cruel. Assuming that he is still living in your home and you are the parent, you are entitled to a say in certain things.

The bottom line is this: Don't play games you can't win.

118 Recognise what not to do in the heat of the moment

None of us get it right every time and, sometimes, when we are angry or tired, the last thing we want to do is avoid conflict. In the heat of the moment it is always better to avoid certain things. For example:

- insults

- bribery

- empty threats

- mentioning contentious things

- sarcasm

- being overbearing

- rhetorical questions such as:

> 'Do you think I enjoy arguing with you like this?' (If he answers you literally you will be even more infuriated with him.)

> 'This is the last time I am going to tell you...' (Again, he may take you literally and drive you mad when he answers with something like 'Thank heavens for that!')

5

Your Relationship with Your Child

Being on the same side
Giving him the benefit of the doubt
Mutual respect

This chapter deals with the all-important relationship between you and your child. It focuses on three main areas:

- Being on the same side (page 96)

- Giving him the benefit of the doubt (page 100)

- Mutual respect (page 104)

BEING ON THE SAME SIDE

TIP BOX

Being on the same side

119   Let it be beyond doubt
120   Tell him in words
121   Believe in him
122   Side with him, not his behaviour
123   Confide and identify
124   Treat confidences with respect
125   Recognise that falling out is not a problem

119 Let it be beyond doubt

It is really important that you are on your child's side, but it is at least as important that he knows this with 100 per cent certainty. Why? For one thing, this is a difficult age, and he may feel he has few other people on his side. But, as well as that, when he is confident that you are on his side he is more likely to be receptive to what you have to say, and that puts you in a better position to influence and help him. If, on the other hand, he does not really believe you are on his side, he is more liable to turn to the wrong people.

120 Tell him in words

Do not assume that he knows you are on his side. You may think this should be obvious. You are his parent after all, you love him very much and you would go to the ends of the earth to help him. But the obvious is not always apparent when you have Asperger Syndrome. He may (like many kids of course) be blind to all you have done for him and take it completely for granted. Sometimes at this age children see their parents mostly as people who get in their way by telling them things they don't want to hear and stopping them from doing things they want to do – and that is even when they don't have Asperger Syndrome! So you may need to spell out the obvious. Tell him, for example:

- that you are on his side and want the best for him

- that because you are older and have experienced more of life than him sometimes you can see round corners to where he cannot see, and you may be aware of dangers and pitfalls which he may not be aware of

- that it is natural at his age for children to want to do things for themselves

- that it is also natural for parents to want to guide and protect them

- that life works much better when people are on the same side as each other instead of being at loggerheads

- that nobody is perfect and no family is perfect, but when family members are on the same side they can do a lot to help and support each other.

121 Believe in him

It can make a huge difference to him to know there is at least one person in his life who believes in him.

122 Side with him, not his behaviour

Being on his side does not mean you have to approve of everything he does. If he does something you think is wrong and you feel you need to tell him, aim to do so in such a way that he understands and respects your opinion, but does not feel you have turned against him personally. Again, you may need to spell this out in words. Be honest about your dilemma if needs be. Tell him you are in a difficult situation, that you want to be on his side but you feel he is making a mistake or being irresponsible. Remind him that being on his side does not mean you like everything he does.

And if you are upset by his behaviour try not to react in a knee jerk way. Don't say dramatic things that you will regret such as 'You are no son of mine', 'I am finished with you.' Don't forget he will probably take your words literally and remember them. You know in your heart that words run deep.

123 Confide and identify

Nurture the bond with your child by confiding in him when appropriate in such a way that he realises you have a lot in common and that you think enough of him to trust him with your confidences. Identify with him where you can. For example, if he has a problem with motivation, admit that you have similar problems sometimes. Or that you used to when you were younger and have been able to improve. This can help affirm the idea that you are on the same side, and it can give him an optimistic hope and a vision about himself and his potential to take on and master certain traits within himself.

Confiding with him about your own problems can also be a good way to pass suggestions on to him without appearing to be controlling or interfering. Say, for example:

'Yeah, I have that problem too sometimes.'

'One thing I find helpful is...'

'Have you found anything helpful?'

'Why do you think that works?'

124 Treat confidences with respect

When your child confides in you, especially about something that reveals himself as vulnerable in some way, see this as an honour and a privilege. Tell him you want to treat his confidence with respect, and discuss generally issues such as confidentiality and discretion. Remember it can be difficult for any of us to be real; and it can be even more difficult when you are a young person with Asperger Syndrome. His confiding in you is a mark of his trust in you, and he deserves you to honour that trust.

125 Recognise that falling out is not a problem

You are bound to fall out with each other sometimes. Make sure he does not get this out of proportion and that he understands how these things work. The important issue is not whether you fall out so much as how you resolve your differences afterwards. Sometimes when people fall out, issues which need attention come to the surface. Lessons can be learned and you can move on to a better relationship.

Helping him to see these things can lead to a discussion about the concept of forgiveness, and you might find yourself surprised and interested at what he has to say – the viewpoint of people with AS is often original and thought-provoking.

GIVING HIM THE BENEFIT OF THE DOUBT

TIP BOX

Giving him the benefit of the doubt

126   He is probably unaware of how he comes across
127   He usually does not intend to cause offence
128   He usually wants to get it right
129   'The obvious' is not always so obvious!

126 He is probably unaware of how he comes across

When you don't understand AS very well, it is easy to jump to the wrong conclusion. But that can be very unfair, because people with AS are usually not aware of how they come across; for example, they usually have no intention of appearing arrogant, rude or unpleasant. Your child has probably had more than his fair share of harsh judgement from the world. The last thing he needs is for his parents to judge him in the same harsh way.

There are some very good reasons why he deserves you to give him the benefit of the doubt, for example:

- He usually does not intend to cause offence (see 127 below, and Tips 53–64).

- He is naive and vulnerable socially (see Tips 74–85).

- He may be less (or more) capable than you think (see Tips 35–43).

- He is probably a perfectionist – generally driven to 'get it right' – and will tend to feel like a failure if he thinks he is 'getting it wrong' or making mistakes (see Tips 65–73).

- He may not know 'the obvious' (see Tip 129).

- He may not understand 'the obvious' (see Tip 129).

- He may not remember 'the obvious' (see Tip 129).

- He may not think of saying 'the obvious' (see Tips 129 and 53–64).

127 He usually does not intend to cause offence

One of the problems faced by Aspies is that they are not necessarily good at doing things which might make them likeable. In fact the way they come across can sometimes give a completely wrong impression – that they are deliberately setting out to cause offence or get people's backs up. But we know in our hearts that this is not true. Most people, if they are honest about it, would prefer to be liked than disliked. And it is no different for people with Asperger Syndrome. So, if your child seems to be grumpy and abrasive, the reason may be that he is unhappy about something and cannot manage to express it, or perhaps he is unaware of how he is coming across and does not 'get it'. Either way he deserves you to give him the benefit of the doubt.

128 He usually wants to get it right

Another problem faced by Aspies is that they seem constantly to be 'getting it wrong' and failing to meet other people's expectations – academically, socially and so on but, again, it is unfair to assume they are not doing their best. In fact an intrinsic part of Aspergers is often a drive to get things right, and it must be very hard for your child to be constantly getting the message that he is getting things wrong. So it is only fair to give him the benefit of the doubt and assume his good intention, until proved otherwise. People with AS prefer to be successful and happy just like anyone else.

129 'The obvious' is not always so obvious!

Don't make assumptions about your child's state of mind and awareness based on what you consider to be 'obvious'. People with AS are often tuned in to different things from most other people. Bear in mind that he may not always know, understand, remember or think of saying 'the obvious'.

- *He may not know 'the obvious'.* Let's take a simple example. Imagine you meet a young person with AS for coffee in a coffee bar every week and you end up paying for his coffee each time. You might assume he is being mean, because it is 'obvious' that he should offer to buy you one sometimes. But in reality he may not be tuned in to the social convention that says he should take a turn to buy the coffee.

- *He may not understand 'the obvious'.* If the situation were pointed out to him, he would probably see the logic and fairness behind the social convention of taking turns, but he may find it harder to understand that his failure to offer to buy coffee could show him up in a bad light or that he might be perceived as rude or mean. Buying or not buying coffee is probably the last thing on his mind when so much of his attention is taken up with processing the social situation in the coffee shop. This kind of situation is probably nothing to do with meanness. It is not uncommon among Aspies who are otherwise extremely generous.

- *He may not remember 'the obvious'.* To take the coffee example a stage further, let's imagine that you make the effort to patiently explain the social conventions and expectations to your child. Even if he logically understands and accept what you are saying, the issue may be so unimportant to him that the next time he goes to the coffee shop he once again forgets to offer to pay!

- *He may not think of saying 'the obvious'.* And when you meet him the following week and something important has happened to him during the week, do not assume he will think of telling you. Even if the event is major and significant and it happened to him the very day before, there is a fair chance that he will not tell you, even if you ask him if he has any news. Why? Possibly because he may not remember. The Asperger memory can be a strange one to figure out. Sometimes Aspies find it hard to access data from their memory bank, and are literally unable to bring it to mind at a specific moment. And sometimes it does not occur to them to say 'the obvious'.

MUTUAL RESPECT

TIP BOX

Mutual respect

130 It starts with self-respect
131 It's for his sake too
132 Meet him where he is at
133 It's the little things that count
134 Discuss earning respect
135 'If it matters to you...'
136 Respect his decisions
137 Keep your word
138 Step back
139 Respect his passion
140 Support his dreams and visions

130 It starts with self-respect

It is easier to elicit respect from people when you respect yourself. That's the simple truth. When you have a healthy self-respect, it will emanate from you in such a way that your child cannot help picking it up. That kind of dynamic is good for him and gives him a wholesome example for his own life.

When you have self-respect you naturally challenge your child any time he is disrespectful – you do not let yourself be verbally bullied, for example. And when you notice a conversation heading in a particular direction you put the brakes on, for example, by saying simply 'I don't want to discuss this', 'No, I don't have to give you a reason', 'I am ending this conversation', 'I don't like your tone' and so forth.

131 It's for his sake too

It is important that your child respects you – not only because you deserve respect but also because learning respect is good for him. An appropriately respectful attitude will enrich his life and help him appreciate it better. Also he will learn from you more easily when he respects you. And, most importantly, his relationship with you can be a model for how he relates to other people in life.

132 Meet him where he is at

In our relationship with our child we want to give him a model of how things should ideally be. We want to give him an example of how to treat others and how he deserves to be treated himself. But no young person wants to feel patronised. To encourage him to accept your view of the world, you really need to meet him where he is at, take an interest in his world view and accept that how he sees things is how he sees things. When you start from that perspective, hopefully over time he will become more open to your way of seeing things as well so that over time mutual respect will naturally evolve.

133 It's the little things that count

Mutual respect can be taught in many ways – even small things like taking turns and speaking in a respectful tone of voice. Model these things in your family so that he gets a good example. Think of how you talk to complete strangers. There is no reason for family members to speak to each other with less courtesy!

134 Discuss earning respect

Talk to your child about the issue of respect. Explain how your hard work and dedication as a parent entitles you to respect, and discuss all the ways in which respect can be earned. Talk about how he can earn – and has already earned – your respect, for example, by his efforts, attitude to life, courage, kindness and so on.

135 'If it matters to you...'

Encourage your child to talk to you by taking an interest in what interests him and taking his opinions and concerns seriously. Gradually, over time, you should find that he will start to respect and take an interest in what's important to you as well.

136 Respect his decisions

Naturally we do not like to see our children making mistakes, but sometimes it is better to respect their autonomy and allow them to make small mistakes and learn from them. If you protect him from making too many small mistakes he may feel controlled and be more likely to rebel when it comes to major choices and decisions. As always, it may be helpful to explain things clearly. Let him know for example that you have decided to respect his decision in this situation, and that it is important for people to respect each other's opinions even if they do not necessarily agree with them.

137 Keep your word

Encourage mutual respect by being reliable, keeping your promises and expecting the same standard from him in return.

138 Step back

Sometimes we can be overly controlling or over-protective with our children without realising it – especially in the circumstances where they have needed a lot of extra help and intervention when they were small and we have had to be very involved. Part of the process of adolescence involves us letting go of control. Remember, it is his life, and you will probably not always be there. Aim to put the ball in his court where possible.

139 Respect his passion

During adolescence young people with AS can feel lost and aimless. Help your child understand that everyone has something to contribute and a unique purpose in life. What is his passion? Does he have one? Perhaps he used to have and he has temporarily forgotten about it. Maybe you can help him find it again. What was he interested in when he was younger? Did he have a special interest? Questions like these can help move him in the direction of finding where his heart lies.

140 Support his dreams and visions

Perhaps your child has a dream or vision about his future. And perhaps he is keeping it to himself. Or perhaps he needs a bit of encouragement to come up with some sort of vision for his future. It can take time to figure these things out, but that doesn't matter. In the meantime support his dreams. Don't belittle him even if his ideas about career and so forth seem daft and unrealistic at the moment. These things work out over time (see also Tips 265–79). He will get there in the end!

6

Self-Image

Encourage him to have a positive self-regard
Encourage him to have a positive attitude to Asperger Syndrome
Help shape core beliefs

This chapter looks at issues which can affect your child's self-image. In particular how we can:

- Encourage him to have a positive self-regard (page 110)
- Encourage him to have a positive attitude to Asperger Syndrome (page 114)
- Help shape core beliefs (page 118)

  'I'm ok'

  'I don't need to be perfect'

  'I am doing well'

  'I matter'

  'I am worth getting to know'

  'I am a valuable human being'

  'I deserve to be treated with respect'

  'I am capable of facing and dealing with challenges'

  'I have hope and a vision for my future'

ENCOURAGE HIM TO HAVE A POSITIVE SELF-REGARD

TIP BOX

Encourage him to have a positive self-regard

141 Remember Lily's secret

142 Be proud of him – and make sure he knows it!

143 Look for opportunities

144 Recognise the power of praise

145 Use the past tense method

146 Use the positive sandwich technique

147 Change is possible

See also Tips 157–75.

141 Remember Lily's secret

There have been many experts involved in my son's life ever since he was young. They have done a lot to help and I have learned a lot from them, but by far the most crucial lesson I have ever learned came from Lily.

Lily is not an expert (at least not in the sense of having any impressive sounding qualifications) but she is a very special lady, and she has made a crucial difference in Kenneth's life. And in case you are wondering, Lily is actually my mother-in-law!

When Lily first met Kenneth he was a grumpy, difficult teen and he and I were not getting on well. He did not want to bother with anyone, and he could come across as surly, rude and unfriendly. But Lily did not seem to mind or even to notice this. She saw him differently. She kept telling me what a lovely young man Kenneth was and how much she loved him! And she 'spoiled' him the way Grannies do sometimes. And gradually, over time, with the help of her love, I saw Kenneth become far more happy and relaxed, and many things began slowly to improve.

So what is Lily's secret? I've been trying to figure it out; and here's my take on it – Lily firmly believes in the power of love, and she knows how to make a person feel good about himself – wanted, loved and accepted. That's the bottom line, for that kind of energy can be very transformative. She has a heart for unusual and slightly eccentric people, and she does the little things in a larger than life way so that her message is clear and unambiguous. For example, every time she sees Kenneth she greets him very warmly, hugs him and tells him how glad she is to see him. These things may be small but they are far more important than we realise.

Lily helps me remember that self-esteem is crucial. When you have good positive self-esteem, you feel good about who you are at a deep level, and this impacts many aspects of your life. You are generally happier, more confident and you are more likely to find your place in the world and feel successful. And, although it is not always obvious, people with AS often have low self-esteem. We can do a lot to help simply by relating to them in a warm, loving way.

And what does Lily think her secret is? When I asked her, this is what she told me.

> 'Just make sure he knows he is loved. It's all about the little things. Like hugs... And plenty of chocolate!'

142 Be proud of him – and make sure he knows it!

When your child feels like you are proud of him, this allows him to be proud of himself, and he feels like a million dollars. The best way to let him know you are proud of him without appearing patronising is often just to notice his efforts and remark on them in a matter-of-fact way. Simply telling him that you notice can make all the difference.

Something as simple as 'I notice you have completed your assignment, well done!', for example. And, as he gets older, acknowledging that your relationship with each other is improving can make him proud in a good and healthy way too. Just tell him, for example 'I notice we are getting on better as you get older.'

He deserves to be proud of who he is – and Aspergers is part of who he is, so ideally he will be proud of his Aspergers too (see also Tips 148–56).

143 Look for opportunities

The question to keep uppermost in your mind in every situation and interaction involving your child is this one: 'Will this enhance or diminish his self-esteem?'

144 Recognise the power of praise

When a child is young, praise can be a useful tool to help shape his behaviour. The general principle is that it is better to 'catch him doing something right' and reinforce that, rather than ignore him until he is doing something 'wrong' and draw attention to that. And the principle is exactly the same for adolescents and young adults. The only difference is in the manner of delivery.

Praise for this age group needs to be a lot more subtle. They do not respond well to feedback that seems gushing, over the top or insincere.

145 Use the past tense method

One good way to make use of the power of praise is to use the 'past tense method'. How this works is that you identify the changes you would like to see in your child and keep a close eye out for them. And when you see even a glimpse of a desirable change starting to happen, this can be an opportunity to use the past tense method.

For example, most adolescent Aspies go through periods of being very surly and grumpy. This might go on for a very long time, and you long for the day when he might be a bit more pleasant. Nagging him to 'stop being grumpy' doesn't usually work. Instead wait for the day when for whatever reason he is in great form and you see a different side to him – pleasant and smiley and upbeat. This is your chance to use the past tense method. Reinforce his more cheerful state of mind and demeanour by saying something like, 'It's great to see the way you're becoming more friendly these days. Remember you used to be so grumpy!' (You need to say it in an upbeat, light-hearted way, of course!)

146 Use the positive sandwich technique

If you have something critical or negative to say to your child, try putting it in a 'positive sandwich'. In other words, say something positive before and afterwards.

147 Change is possible

Don't dwell on your child's problems and shortcomings by talking about them too much. Encourage him to see himself as someone who is capable of making change and improvement over time.

ENCOURAGE HIM TO HAVE A POSITIVE ATTITUDE TO ASPERGER SYNDROME

TIP BOX

Encourage him to have a positive attitude to Asperger Syndrome

148 Encourage him to be Aspie and proud of it!
149 Your attitude matters
150 Examine your attitude to AS
151 Develop an appreciation for AS
152 Explore the positives
153 Remember that Aspies are not boring!
154 Encourage positive role models
155 Let AS help you learn about yourself
156 Encourage a fair press

148 Encourage him to be Aspie and proud of it!

There is a lot about AS that is great. Aspies are interesting, quirky individuals, with original slants and points of view. Their unusual attitude to life can be inspiring as well as challenging. But in reality we often end up focusing on the problems associated with AS and becoming very negative about it. It is necessary to focus on problems in order to try to find solutions of course, but overall we need to see AS in a positive light in order to help our children do the same.

AS is an integral part of your child – it is vital that he feels positively about it.

149 Your attitude matters

You can influence your child's attitude in various ways: by your attitude, by drawing attention to positive aspects and some positive role models; and by sharing with him how learning about AS is helping you learn about yourself. He will learn a lot from:

- how you talk to him about AS
- how he hears you talk to others
- what you say and how you say it
- if you have your own Asperger traits, whether you talk about them freely or are in denial.

150 Examine your attitude to AS

If you are very worried or disappointed that your child has AS, it is better to admit this to yourself. But here's a challenging thought: If you wish your child didn't have AS, then in a way you are wishing he was someone different. So is it your child you love or some fantasy version of him?

Be honest with yourself. How do you really feel about your child's Aspergers? For he will pick this up. Are you proud? Or are you embarrassed, ashamed or disappointed? Perhaps you need to grieve for the child you *wish* he was or you thought he was going to be. If so, you might want to consider intervention such as counselling in order to help you come to terms with reality. This might be a loving and constructive thing to do.

If you are finding your child's AS hard to accept, don't feel guilty about it. The world can be a difficult place for people with AS and it is natural to worry about him and wish you could change things. If you are suppressing some negative emotions, try to bring them to consciousness, deal with them and move on. Hopefully this will allow you to accept and appreciate him for the wonderful, precious person he really is.

151 Develop an appreciation for AS

The world needs Asperger Syndrome! It has been associated with many brilliant and creative people throughout history. People with AS tend to be original thinkers, but life can be a real struggle for them. When you understand some of their struggle, it can help you appreciate their strengths and admire their courage. Think about these things in relation to your child and take pleasure in getting to know and understand him more deeply across time as he develops and becomes an unusual, individual and very interesting adult.

152 Explore the positives

Point out to your child that:

- The world needs Asperger Syndrome. Many of the core traits of AS have been essential to man's achievements and progress throughout history.

- Everyone has some Asperger-type tendencies, and the AS parts of people are often the most interesting!

- People with AS are individual thinkers who work out their own values, and this can be very refreshing.

- The world these days is much more suitable than it has ever been for Aspies. There is much more awareness than there used to be, and the internet age opens doors to possibilities which were not there before.

153 Remember that Aspies are not boring!

Think about it this way – Asperger Syndrome is a fascinating condition and your child is far from boring. When you have this attitude your child will pick this up and feel better about himself.

154 Encourage positive role models

Encourage your child to do some research into inspiring AS role models – gifted and talented Aspies. Look at your family and identify traits among family members even if they are not diagnosed. There are some online Autism Quizzes available which can be interesting and fun (if you Google 'Asperger Quiz' lots of ideas will come up)!

155 Let AS help you learn about yourself

Discuss with your child the possibility that exploring and embracing your own Aspie parts might help you learn more about yourself and change or liberate you as an individual.

156 Encourage a fair press

Sometimes Asperger Syndrome gets a bad press, mostly because unfortunately people like to focus on things that are sensational and negative. And while Aspergers is a very complex and wide ranging condition, and full of extremes, usually Aspies who display behaviour at the more troublesome extreme get most of the attention, while those at the opposite extreme are overlooked and ignored.

Perhaps there are people who are diagnosed with Asperger Syndrome who are in some way bad or evil. If so, personally I have never met them, and my experience leads me to believe that the opposite is true, for in general people with Asperger Syndome are more likely than average to hold themselves to their own internal standards of integrity and courage, and these standards can be exceptionally high.

HELP SHAPE CORE BELIEFS

TIP BOX

Help shape core beliefs

157 Plant seeds
158 Make words matter
159 Take a 'no strings' approach
160 Nobody can be good at everything!
161 Explain the jagged profile
162 Emphasise that mistakes are for learning
163 Encourage him to play to his strengths
164 Tell him you've noticed the effort he is making
165 Practise 'holding a mirror' up to each other
166 Give the gift of time
167 Take an interest in his interests
168 Say that you enjoy his company
169 Tell him that you cherish his individuality
170 Create happy memories
171 Let him know that you want his input
172 Tell him you will be sensitive
173 Let him know that he can make changes
174 Confidence comes in baby steps
175 His future is full of hope

157 Plant seeds

If only we realised. The messages we give our children shape their core beliefs about who they are in a very profound and far reaching way. They plant seeds which may bear fruit for many years to come.

Can you think of some things your parents said to you when you were younger which made you feel either good or bad about yourself? Even if you can't bring them to mind immediately, there will be things they said (or didn't say) which will have gone in deep and contributed in a powerful way to the person you are today, how you relate to the world and what you believe about yourself at a core level.

Aim to pass on to your child the following core beliefs:

'You are OK.' (Tips 158–9)

'You don't need to be perfect.' (Tips 160–2)

'You are doing well.' (Tips 163–5)

'You matter.' (Tips 166–7)

'You are worth getting to know.' (Tips 169–70)

'You are a valuable human being.' (Tips 168–9)

'You have a valuable contribution to make.' (Tip 171)

'You deserve to be treated with respect.' (Tip 172)

'You are capable of dealing with life.' (Tip 173)

'Your future is full of hope.' (Tip 174–5)

158 Make words matter

You do not always have to tell your child in words what he needs to hear, but you need to be very clear in your own mind what the core beliefs are that you want to pass on. That way you will naturally pass on the right messages which will shape his core beliefs. But there will be moments which come along when you will have the opportunity to tell him who he is by using words, and you need to be ready for those moments.

Words are powerful. Be careful about what you say to your child and what he overhears you say about him. Be especially careful in heated moments, when you are at the end of your tether, that you do not say things you will regret. Sharp or cruel words can cut very deep, especially when those words come from someone he trusts, and when they are voicing his own deep inner fears.

159 Take a 'no strings' approach

It is good to congratulate achievement, especially if it has come as a result of hard work and effort, but be careful your child's self-esteem is not too tied up in his skills or achievements, because that can set him up for disappointment in the future and he can take it very badly if he sees himself as failing or making a mistake.

Your child needs to know: 'You are a unique, valuable human being and I you love you for who you are. My love for you is not conditional upon anything you do or don't do, and it is not conditional upon you "doing well" in the world.'

160 Nobody can be good at everything!

Your child needs to know: 'If you have difficulties with certain things, that is not so unusual. Everybody finds some things easier than others.'

161 Explain the jagged profile

Your child needs to know: 'AS is a developmental disorder, and that is good news and bad news. The bad news is that at any given time you are liable to be out of step with your peers – ahead in some respects and behind in others. The good news is that you can keep learning for the rest of your life, and that learning can make life challenging and interesting. And if you put your mind to it, you can not only catch up, but even overtake in many areas, if you have the right attitude.'

162 Emphasise that mistakes are for learning

Your child needs to know: 'There is no reason to feel bad if you make a mistake. Mistakes are part of life and we can learn a lot from them. The intelligent thing to do is to embrace your mistakes as learning opportunities – everybody makes mistakes. That's why they put rubbers at the end of pencils!'

163 Encourage him to play to his strengths

Your child needs to know: 'There is no reason to feel down on yourself just because there are certain things you find very difficult. Accept those things and know you can work steadily on them over time and make progress. But it is smart to home in your strong points. What are they? It can be fulfilling and satisfying to find things to do which make the best of your individual skills.'

164 Tell him you've noticed the effort he is making

Your child needs to know: 'I see the effort that you are making in life, even if I do not tell you all the time. I know that many things are not easy for you and I admire you for the effort you make.'

165 Practise 'holding a mirror' up to each other

Your child needs to know: 'Nobody ever has a completely clear picture of how they appear to the world or of the impact they have on other people. And when you have Asperger Syndrome this may be even more true.

When people love and trust each other sometimes they can hold a mirror up, so to speak, and help each other to see themselves as others see them.

As your parent I would like to hold a mirror up to you sometimes, because it could be helpful for you to have more information about how you present yourself to the world. That means that sometimes I will appear to be criticising you, but I will try to do this in the spirit of kindness and for the right reasons, and I will not force my opinions on you.

And perhaps you can hold a mirror up for me too sometimes!'

166 Give the gift of time
Your child needs to know: 'You are important to me and I have time for you. Spending time with you is important enough to me and I enjoy including you in my plans. One of the most valuable gifts we can give each other is to enjoy time in each other's company.'

167 Take an interest in his interests
Your child needs to know: 'You count. Your feelings, opinions and interests matter to me and I want to listen to what you have to say.'

168 Say that you enjoy his company
Your child needs to know: 'I have interests and responsibilities that inevitably take up my time but I enjoy spending time with you and value your company.'

169 Tell him that you cherish his individuality
Your child needs to know: 'I am glad you are who you are. You are an interesting person and an original thinker and that's cool with me. I like the way you challenge my thinking and I am interested in your take on life.'

170 Create happy memories

Your child needs to know: 'When I look back on your childhood, certain moments stand out as very happy memories. Maybe right now we can create some happy memories and one day we will be looking back on those too.'

171 Let him know that you want his input

Your child needs to know: 'You are better than me at some things these days (possibly computer skills!). I would appreciate your opinion, advice or help in those areas sometimes.'

172 Tell him you will be sensitive

Your child needs to know: 'You do not deserve to be put in situations that cause you humiliation or embarrassment and I will try to make sure this does not happen.'

173 Let him know that he can make changes

Your child needs to know: 'You are capable of making changes in your life if and when you need or want to, and I am willing to help you if I can.'

174 Confidence comes in baby steps

Your child needs to know: 'I understand that life can sometimes knock your confidence, especially when you have Asperger Syndrome, but you can learn to be truly confident. I would like to help you but ultimately you need to grow your own confidence. It is not easy, but you deserve to be confident and you have what it takes.

True confidence is something that grows slowly and gradually, and it takes effort and courage. To become more confident sometimes you may need to step out of your comfort zone and knowingly risk failure, and that takes guts. And sometimes, when you make such an effort, you will be disappointed and think you have made a fool of yourself. That doesn't matter. What matters is that you had the courage to try, that you will not let setbacks stand in your way and that you will keep trying.'

175 His future is full of hope

Your child needs to know: 'Life can be an interesting and fun journey, if you choose to see it that way, and you will have many choices to make as you grow older. To a large extent you are the master of your own destiny. I believe in you and you must believe in yourself.'

7

Communication that Works

Ready to listen, ready to talk
Clear, honest and direct communication

How we communicate with our children can make a huge difference. We can help by being:

- Ready to listen, ready to talk (page 126)

Ideally they need:

- Clear, honest and direct communication (page 131)

READY TO LISTEN, READY TO TALK

TIP BOX

Ready to listen, ready to talk

176 Make one-to-one time
177 Communication can't be forced
178 Make friends before you make points
179 Think quantity then quality
180 Don't be put off
181 Talk to him, not at him
182 Agree to turn phones off
183 Don't pry
184 Say 'Tell me more about that'
185 Be there

176 Make one-to-one time

Aspies usually find it easier to talk and open up in a one-to-one setting. Set aside and plan one-to-one time with your child, especially if he is quiet and withdrawn.

177 Communication can't be forced

Rather than try to force your child to listen to you, aim to create a climate where he *wants* to talk to you openly and honestly and where he will listen to what you have to say. This is most likely to happen when you spend quality time together and where he perceives you as receptive and ready to listen to him. Then, when the channels of communication are open, he will be more likely to listen to anything you have to say to him.

178 Make friends before you make points

When people perceive each other as friends or allies they are likely to communicate better than if they perceive each other as rivals or enemies. This is a sound principle and worth bearing in mind in relation to your child. If there is an ongoing problem or dispute between you, try to resolve it before expecting much constructive communication.

179 Think quantity then quality

We all know that quality time with our children is a good idea. When we think of quality time the picture that comes to mind is one of harmony and trust. We enjoy each other's company and we can be real with each other about the things that matter to us.

During quality time your child is more likely to listen to you and confide in you, but of course trust does not happen overnight; it takes time to build. So be prepared: you may need to spend a considerable *quantity* of time together before it evolves into *quality* time.

180 Don't be put off

People with AS often communicate in ways that make other people uncomfortable. For example, there is a fair chance that your child is at one or other extreme in terms of how much he talks.

He may either talk a lot, to the point that other people find him boring or overbearing. Or he may talk very little, to the point where other people feel uncomfortable around him. There may be long silences, leaving them struggling to find the right questions to ask to get a decent conversation going. And this can seem too much like hard work! And at either extreme Aspies often communicate in a blunt, direct and matter-of-fact way which other people find abrasive.

Even if things like this make communication with your child uncomfortable for you, don't be put off, and try to persevere anyway.

181 Talk to him, not at him

Talking *to* your child rather than *at* him means having a real dialogue where each of you takes it in turns to talk and then truly listen to the other. That's all very well in theory of course, but in reality listening is not always easy. And I'm sure all of us at some point have found ourselves in the position where instead of really listening to our children (or anyone else for that matter!) and considering carefully what they have to say, we are really preparing what we are going to say next – figuring out what we are going to say just as soon as we can find a gap in the conversation!

If this sounds familiar, a 'conch' might be a fun way to encourage more effective talking and listening in your family. In reality a conch is a large seashell which can be blown to make a trumpeting sound. In *The Lord of the Flies* (Golding 2012[1954]) a conch was blown to call people to important meetings. And to keep meetings orderly, the conch was held by the person speaking at the time. The idea was that only that person could speak, while the others were supposed to listen.

When used as a communication device in the context suggested here, a conch can be any agreed object which has to be held by whoever is speaking. Any person who is not holding the conch cannot speak till it is his turn to hold it. The conch can be any object you want it to be – perhaps a beanbag – even a banana if you like!

Using a conch can encourage people who talk too much to talk less and listen more, and vice versa (see also Tips 311–13).

182 Agree to turn phones off

Make a pact. Either for a one-to-one situation or for a family get together, agree in advance that for a specified amount of time, say even half an hour, each person turns off his mobile phone or puts it on silent, sets it face down in the middle of the table and makes an effort to talk and listen to each other.

Get rid of other distractions such as TV as well and agree some kind of reward – perhaps something as simple as a cup of tea and some cake, for when the half hour is up. Whoever looks at their phone first has to make the tea!

183 Don't pry

It is not unusual for a young person to be secretive at this age and to hide his inner feelings. Respect his privacy and do not pry, unless you have a really good reason.

184 Say 'Tell me more about that'

Sometimes you may find your child talking enthusiastically about something which you have little interest in or which you know very little about, but he gets into lots of detail anyway. It is as if he assumes that (1) you are just as interested as him and (2) you have as much background knowledge and understanding of the subject matter as he does.

This kind of conversation can go off the rails a bit when you try too hard to keep up with him. Like anyone else, sometimes all he wants is a listening ear, and when you ask the wrong question, he can get frustrated because it is obvious that you are not following what he is saying.

For times like this it can be helpful to have a few scripts up your sleeve. For example, 'That sounds interesting' or 'Tell me more about that.'

185 Be there

There will be times when you are concerned about your child because you know he is going through something tough or painful, but instead of talking to you or anyone else about it, he withdraws. At times like these, there may be no point in trying to force conversation. He will probably be glad of some TLC though, and there is no harm in telling him in words that you are there for him if he feels like a chat.

Ask is there anything you can do to help. If he says no, leave it at that for the moment. Just tell him, 'OK, but if you think of anything let me know.'

CLEAR, HONEST AND DIRECT COMMUNICATION

TIP BOX

Clear, honest and direct communication

186 Spell things out
187 Make expectations clear
188 C and R (Clarify and Repeat)
189 Don't overload
190 Be calm and logical
191 Use humour carefully
192 Don't be a know-it-all
193 Don't pretend to be perfect
194 Help him to understand socially acceptable lies
195 Love without honesty...

186 Spell things out

Aspies have a reputation for being direct and honest, and your child needs you to communicate with him in a way that reflects his natural way of being and takes it into account. Remember, clear, honest and direct communication is easier and less tiring for him to process and understand. There is not much room for hints and subtlety!

He may need you to spell out things which seem obvious to other people, explain them clearly and make sure he has understood. If you can put him in the picture about what other people might be thinking or intending and help him know where he stands, this can relieve a lot of stress and confusion, which can be a real gift to him.

187 Make expectations clear

Explain to him in words very clearly the things he needs to know such as what is expected to happen and what other people expect from him.

188 C and R (Clarify and Repeat)

To prevent too many misunderstandings, sometimes the clarify and repeat technique can be useful. Ask him to repeat back to you what you have just told him, in his own words, so you know he has heard it accurately. You can also do the same for him when appropriate, to help him realise you have listened to him and understood what he has said. This technique has the additional advantage of reinforcing communication.

If either of you is trying to explain something that the other is having great difficulty understanding, take the C and R step by step. Repeat what has been said slowly and patiently and get step by step feedback on whether it has been heard and understood accurately.

189 Don't overload

Make allowances for processing differences: Be vigilant and sensitive during conversation, and gauge whether your child is still plugged in. If he has tuned out it may be because you have bombarded him with too much information, or because you have expected him to process too much too quickly. If so, ease off. Do not fall into the trap of adding more information to the mix in an effort to make things clearer. Let it go.

If you think he is getting overloaded and needs more processing time, there is no harm in saying so in a light and matter-of-fact way: 'That's a lot to think about. You probably need time to think it over.'

190 Be calm and logical

As a rule of thumb, it is generally best to keep things calm and reasonable, appeal to logic and avoid emotional drama.

191 Use humour carefully

When it comes to humour, Aspies tend to fall towards either end of two extremes. They may have a keen and highly developed sense of humour or the opposite. You know your own child, so you know which extreme he falls at. Either way it is better to be cautious and tread carefully with humour such as sarcasm, especially if your child is feeling vulnerable. It is possible that he might take your words completely literally.

192 Don't be a know-it-all

It is good for your child to see you as a figure of authority and respect you, but it is also good sometimes for him to see that you do not know everything, and you are not trying to pretend you do. There is no harm sometimes in saying 'I don't know.' Hopefully he will respect this as an honest admission, and it may offer the opportunity for the two of you to investigate or research something together and perhaps have in interesting discussion about it.

193 Don't pretend to be perfect

To earn respect you don't have to pretend you are perfect. Be prepared to acknowledge your own strengths and weaknesses in a matter-of-fact way; and to admit when you are wrong. Rather than appearing weak, your honesty can inspire his admiration and trust.

194 Help him to understand socially acceptable lies

One of the things that makes communication difficult for your child is that people with AS are not naturally tuned in to a lot of unspoken social rules. For example that there are certain 'lies' that are OK in the sense that they are generally socially acceptable. You may be able to help him figure this out and come to terms with it. To this end, you could talk to him about the concept of honesty. It might end up being an extremely interesting conversation and perhaps the first of many such interesting conversations!

Help him understand that honesty is a very worthy aim, but that nobody is perfectly honest. And that there is a range of 'lies' that are more or less acceptable socially, for example:

- euphemisms

- white lies

- compliments

- approximations

- ignoring 'elephants in the room'.

Discuss with him:

- the reasons for socially acceptable lies, other than the intention to deceive (for example, the wish to avoid giving offence)

- the idea that the world is an uncomfortable place if you don't play the social game; and often the world doesn't reward honesty. Does he agree?

- the idea that a lot of great art, poetry, comedy, etc. works *because* people recognise its honesty and because it says things that people do not usually say (unless they have Asperger Syndrome, of course!).

195 Love without honesty...

There may be times when love requires you to be honest with your child, even when you know that honesty is going to hurt. Bad news can sometimes be easier than no news and in certain situations it is better for him to know where he stands. The ideal is to balance love and honesty – to be honest, but at the same time sensitive and careful about causing hurt, offence or upset.

Remember: Love without honesty is sentimentality, but honesty without love is just brutality.

8

A Predictable World?

Understanding control versus chaos
Encouraging order and structure
Setting boundaries and limits

Your child needs a certain level of predictability in his world but may find it hard to create this for himself. You can help him by:

- Understanding control versus chaos (page 138)

- Encouraging order and structure (page 142)

- Setting boundaries and limits (page 148)

UNDERSTANDING CONTROL VERSUS CHAOS

TIP BOX

Understanding control versus chaos

196 Learn about the systemising brain
197 Understand control and chaos
198 Find out about Asperger life coaching
199 Recognise difficulties coming to light
200 Minimise uncertainty
201 Let go of control
202 Understand MOB – The focus
203 Understand MOB – The benefits
204 Make sense of The Problem with People

See also Tips 224–40.

196 Learn about the systemising brain

The Asperger brain is a systemising brain, according to Simon Baron-Cohen (2002) – it has a great tendency, or perhaps a need, to put information and data into order in a very systematic way.

It is impossible to know for certain why this is. Perhaps it is a way to try to impose control in a world that seems chaotic and hard to predict. But, whatever the reason, you can help your child make sense of the world and feel more secure by:

- encouraging order and structure in his life

- providing solid reliable boundaries so that he knows where he stands and can predict the outcome of his choices

- guiding him through the complex world of emotions.

197 Understand control and chaos

Even though people with AS need order in their lives, they often have great difficulty managing their lives in an orderly way. As usual, the situation can be somewhat complicated and involve the two extremes of control and chaos. A young person with AS may be extremely orderly in some respects while extremely chaotic in other respects; there is rarely a happy medium.

He may, for example:

- have a bedroom that is either extremely neat or extremely messy, but rarely somewhere in the middle

- be extremely punctual or the opposite

- have handwriting that is extremely messy or else meticulous and painstaking

- handle homework and school assignments in a diligent, methodical way or else have huge difficulties in meeting deadlines or managing projects which require any degree of planning and organisation.

This can be hard to make sense of, but it is reasonable to assume that it is connected with the systemising brain in some way; and it is worth trying to understand these extremes and identify them in your child.

198 Find out about Asperger life coaching

Someone with AS may crave order and predictability but find it hard to create it for himself. He may have poor organisation skills which can prevent him from achieving his goals. But if he has an extreme need to be in control he may be reluctant to admit it or let anyone else help him, in case he loses that control. That is where Asperger life coaching can be very helpful, because it can help him identify his own goals and get the kind of support that can make all the difference without him feeling he's lost control.

199 Recognise difficulties coming to light

Difficulties with order may only come to light at around the age of adolescence when academic expectations change and your child is expected to do independent research, produce assignments, meet deadlines and so on.

200 Minimise uncertainty

You cannot make the world totally predictable for your child of course, but you can take away as much uncertainty as you know makes sense. Make a point of talking things through with him with the aim of helping him to know what to expect, what is expected from him and predict the outcome of his choices.

201 Let go of control

None of us like to think we are controlling, but you may have needed to become extremely involved in your child's life when he was young as a result of his difficulties. If so, you may have become used to being in control more than you realise. It is really not so surprising. Children with AS need a lot of attention and help, so you have become very involved for good reasons. But when we get used to being in control, sometimes it can be hard to let go!

At this age it is very important for your child to start to take more control and responsibility over his life. He needs you to gradually step back and hand over the reins. Ultimately it will be up to him to create and maintain moderation, order and balance in his own life.

202 Understand MOB – The focus

Focus on *Moderation, Order* and *Balance* as your child's goals. These are good goals for anyone really, but they are particularly important for people with AS because they have a tendency to become extreme and obsessive, and their approach to life may be either rigid or chaotic. Use the acronym MOB to help you focus on these goals.

203 Understand MOB – The benefits

Help your child see the benefits of moderation, order and balance as goals in his life: that they can help him manage his life, keep things in proportion and reduce anxiety. Tell him you want to help him incorporate them into his life – not only because an orderly, structured life will help him in the short term, but also because they will equip him to take the reins eventually and function better as an adult.

204 Make sense of The Problem with People

Other people can be very hard to fathom and predict when you have Asperger Syndrome, but you can do a certain amount to help him make sense of the social and emotional world by teaching him about (1) the Social Curriculum (Tips 224–40), (2) emotions and nonverbal communication (Tips 241–55), and (3) by encouraging positive social experiences so that over time he can learn about people by direct experience (see Chapter 9).

ENCOURAGING ORDER AND STRUCTURE

TIP BOX

Encouraging order and structure

205 Encourage him to structure his own life

206 Help him see the point

207 Make use of technology

208 Understand 'executive function'

209 Use SMART goals

210 Write it down

211 Use prompts and reminders

212 Send a message!

213 Try mind mapping

214 Find the right life coach

215 Nurture healthy traditions or routines

216 Create your own routines

205 Encourage him to structure his own life

Typically when children are young they rely on their parents to create routine for them and then when they reach adolescence things change. They may reject the traditions, routines and customs of their family, at least for a while, and do their own thing instead. Or they may rebel against the whole idea of routine and tradition. But, usually, in the end, as they settle into adulthood, they start to incorporate routine into their life in a new way.

Young adults usually come up with routines of their own. For example their days and weeks may be landmarked by regular events which are connected with their own jobs, hobbies, friends, sports, pastimes and so on. Perhaps they go to the gym each morning at a certain time, or get together with particular friends every week, or on every birthday, etc. And on top of that they usually leave some room for the traditions and routines of their family as well.

But this typical pattern may not happen in quite the same way for a young person with AS. A lot depends upon whether, when it comes to routines, he is at the controlling or the chaotic end of the extreme. At one extreme Aspies can be rigidly attached to family and personal routines, and find it hard to tolerate any deviation from what they see as the established and correct way of doing things. If your child is like this, he should have a good chance of moving through adolescence and on to adulthood, creating and adapting routines himself along the way to suit his own preferences. Even so, there is no harm in keeping an eye on things. You may need to guide him to be a little more flexible from time to time.

Problems are more likely when a young person with AS is at the more chaotic extreme. He may be indifferent or even hostile to customs, routine and tradition from an early age, typically questioning why people must do things at specific times and in specific ways just because everyone else does the same. Alternatively, he may long for routine but find it just about impossible to bring it about.

In either case, if he can learn how to create and maintain some element of wholesome, healthy structure in his own life, this will be a great advantage to him for the rest of his life.

206 Help him see the point

Young people are liable to interpret as interference any efforts from their parents to help them create order and structure. Some of the following suggestions may help to avoid this:

- *Use logic.* Without appropriate help, some adults with Asperger Syndrome have enormous difficulties in establishing and maintaining even basic day-to-day structure in their lives. Help your child see the point of routines: that without them life can be very difficult to manage, and that this has the potential to cause serious problems in the long run.

- *Choose your moment.* Talk to him when the moment is right and in a way that makes it most likely that he will actually listen and take on board what you have to say (see also Tips 176–85).

- *Let some things go.* Even for typical children, the road to independence can be long and bumpy – when your child has AS you can realistically expect it to be longer and bumpier!

- *Be patient.* Your goal is ultimately for him to take responsibility for managing his own life, but it may be a very long-term goal.

- *Don't push too hard.* Sometimes trying too hard to convince and persuade can be counter-productive.

207 Make use of technology

Your child may find technology very useful to help him with personal management. Most young people enjoy using their computers and mobile phones, and there are countless ways in which computer technology can help him create and maintain order and structure.

Most modern mobile phones include as standard a calendar with a scheduling facility and a clock with an alarm, timer and stopwatch. Encourage him to make use of these to plan and manage his time.

There are many other wonderful apps available to download, either free or very cheaply. Encourage him to find and use apps and programmes which will help him with his daily routines, projects, things he has to remember, tasks he has to do and so on.

208 Understand 'executive function'

Make allowances for the problem sometimes associated with Asperger Syndrome which is referred to as 'executive function'. This is a very genuine impairment and in practice it means that people with AS can find it exceptionally difficult to take ideas from the stage of planning through to completion. At adolescence young people with AS can come under great pressure when they are expected to meet deadlines, organise and plan assignments. If they are in employment, they may find it hard to manage and plan tasks and projects. Some of the ideas in Tips 210–14 may be helpful.

209 Use SMART goals

Encourage him to make his goals SMART: Smart, Measurable, Achievable, Realistic and Time-based (Google 'SMART goals' to find more information).

210 Write it down

We all remember things better when we write them down and this is generally even more true for people with Asperger Syndrome. Encourage your child to write down things that he needs to remember. Notebooks and notice boards can be helpful.

211 Use prompts and reminders

Encourage your child to use visual prompts and reminders. For example, if he has something he wants to remember to do, write it on a piece of paper and put it where he will see it – on top of his computer keyboard often works well. Or if he has an errand to do when he goes out, stick a reminder on the front door so he cannot miss it when he leaves the house.

212 Send a message!

If you think your child is liable to forget something, why not try sending him an email or text. He may see the funny side if he is in the same room as you at the time!

213 Try mind mapping

To help him with a complex task such as an educational assignment, try mind mapping software (Google 'mind mapping software' to find more information).

214 Find the right life coach

A life coach who has some specialist knowledge of Asperger Syndrome can be very helpful. The right life coach can encourage the young person to clarify and plan his goals and guide him to take realistic steps towards achieving them, and ultimately help him manage his life and feel more successful.

215 Nurture healthy traditions or routines

It is natural for adolescents to resist too much regimentation, and it is always important not to be too rigid or controlling. At the same time your child may benefit from a certain element of routine in his daily life, and you can encourage this in simple ways. For example you may have a special family meal on a certain day of the week. Or there may be annual festivals which you celebrate in your family or community. Routines like these may help to create a certain amount of predictability.

216 Create your own routines

Some young people with AS have an aversion to conventional customs and celebrations. Maybe you don't blame him because you feel the same way yourself! Either way, why not create and plan your own alternative routines and celebrations and involve your child in them. It's your life! Craft your own day, week, month and so on. Start some new traditions and make them as zany and original as you like. Celebrate the anniversary of some event that is meaningful to your child or your family. Or, if your child has a special interest or hero figure, why not invent a special day that is somehow connected with that?

SETTING BOUNDARIES AND LIMITS

TIP BOX

Setting boundaries and limits

217   Overindulgence is a mistake
218   Agree basic ground rules
219   Create a written contract
220   Rules without relationship mean rebellion
221   Draw a clear line in the sand
222   Be fair, give clear consequences
223   Explain entitlement versus privilege

217 Overindulgence is a mistake

Young people test the boundaries in a big way during adolescence. It's a fact of life! This is true for any young person, but it is even more true when he has Asperger Syndrome. And at this time they need more than ever to discover that the boundaries are solid.

But when your child has AS and you see him have such a hard time at this age, you can feel tempted to make him feel better by overindulging him. This is very understandable. We love our children and we want the best for them; we love to see them happy, and we are naturally protective about them. All these factors come in to play even if your child has every advantage in the world. But when you know your child has a particular difficulty and you perceive him as being at a disadvantage in the world, the likelihood is that you will be tempted to spoil and overindulge him even more.

Overindulgence is a mistake that I'm sure every parent has made at some point, and we do it in many ways. For example, we pamper our children by giving them too much materially. Or we are too lenient with them about their choices and behaviour; we let them have their way because we hate to see them disappointed. And we protect them from reality by picking up the pieces for them when they make poor choices, instead of letting them see the consequences for themselves.

It can be hard to say 'No' sometimes, but we need to remember what we know in our hearts – overindulgence is not kindness. It can lead our children to develop an attitude of entitlement, give them an unrealistic picture of how the world works and set them up for disappointment in the future.

When you think about it, overindulgence is often about making ourselves feel better and giving ourselves an easier life. We are more likely to spoil our children and give them their own way when we are feeling tired or guilty. So aim for parenting that is firm but fair, and try not to spoil your child. It is called 'spoiling' for a reason after all!

218 Agree basic ground rules

Help your child know where he stands by agreeing some basic ground rules about whatever you feel is important and appropriate. There does not need to be too many rules. In fact it is better to have a few simple, sound rules than a series of complicated rules. And the rules do not need to be comprehensive – just knowing that there are rules in place can go some way to help your child feel more secure.

For younger children, it is not so important that rules are mutually agreed, but when your child reaches adolescence it is better that rules are discussed and that you listen to his point of view.

Of course, if it is not possible to reach agreement, you have to have the last word. Seeing his point does not mean you need his approval, but it is worth making an effort to reach agreement if you can. The bottom line is simple: Trying simply to impose rules at this age can be counter-productive.

What you are aiming for ideally is that your child:

- knows clearly what the ground rules are
- feels that you have taken into account his point of view when making the rules
- understands the reason for them
- sees them as logical, fair and reasonable
- can predict the consequences of breaking the rules with 100 per cent certainty.

219 Create a written contract

Consider putting the ground rules and consequences in writing as a kind of contract. Maybe even make it quite official by having it signed and witnessed!

220 Rules without relationship mean rebellion

Rules are not about being cold and controlling – being firm does not mean you have to be cross. And there is little point in trying to set or enforce rules when the relationship with your child has broken down, or the two of you are at complete loggerheads. Even if you 'win' in the short term, he will probably resent you and rebel eventually. Aim to repair the relationship first and then think about rules.

221 Draw a clear line in the sand

Help your child to understand why you have rules. The message he needs to hear from you is: 'I want to help you make sense of the world. There are some boundaries which you must not cross, and I care enough to defend those boundaries.'

Nip unacceptable behaviour in the bud. Be careful not to let standards slip so that you become acclimatised to behaviour and attitudes that are not OK.

222 Be fair, give clear consequences

Aim for consequences that are clear and proportional, and don't give in for an easy life.

223 Explain entitlement versus privilege

Having an attitude of entitlement is not good for any young person in the long run. It leads him to have unrealistically high expectations about life without really taking responsibility for bringing about the things he expects and wants. It can give him a misleading impression about the world and set him up for disappointment in the future.

Keep in mind the difference between privileges and entitlements, and when appropriate talk to your child about them so he learns to know the difference. It might lead to an interesting discussion. For example, he is entitled to have food and shelter. But is he actually entitled to a mobile phone or TV?

Talk to him about these things logically. The bottom line is that you as the parent have certain responsibilities which he does not have – for running the home and paying bills, for example, which is why you have certain privileges that he does not have. You will do your best to ensure that he gets what he is entitled to, but privileges are optional. They can be earned but ultimately they are at your discretion.

9

The Problem with People

The Social Curriculum
Emotions and nonverbal communication
Positive social experiences

People with AS often find other people very difficult to understand and relate to, and their own emotions hard to regulate and understand. You can make your child's life easier in this regard by helping him learn about:

- The Social Curriculum (page 154)

- Emotions and nonverbal communication (page 167)

And by encouraging him to have:

- Positive social experiences (page 175)

THE SOCIAL CURRICULUM

TIP BOX

The Social Curriculum

224 Understand social heaven and hell
225 It's the hardest subject of all
226 To learn is to grow
227 Help him understand the social game
228 There's more than one right answer
229 Help him see the point
230 It's like learning to swim
231 Break it down
232 Analyse social behaviour
233 Start in the shallow pool
234 Approach it like coaching sessions
235 Reflect and rehearse
236 Try using scripts
237 It's the thought that counts
238 Use compliments
239 Help him make amends
240 Great conversationalists can be very quiet!

224 Understand social heaven and hell

From the moment we are born, we seem programmed to respond to the human face more than any other visual stimulus. And throughout life we are tuned in to recognise faces more readily than anything else. We see faces even in the clouds or in random arrangements of dots. We respond to our mother's voice in the womb and follow her eyes as soon as we are born. And as we grow up we learn to relate to other people in ever more complex and sophisticated ways, until by the time we are adults we have formed our own complex web of social relationships. Dealing with and relating to other people is important to us and it serves many functions. And for most people, relationships are what life is all about.

In the natural course of events, we form strong attachments to our primary caregivers when we are young. Then at a young age we learn to play with other children. The nature of this play changes gradually as we grow, and even though the stages of play development vary between individuals, generally it runs along fairly predictable lines. Then during adolescence, relationships with people of our own age become very important to us. We tend to form strong bonds and alliances among our peer group, and we become interested in romantic and sexual relationships. Finally, by the time we become adults, relationships are still extremely important to us, and we usually have a complex network of human relationships in our lives.

In a typical picture, we have a kind of inner circle of relationships which might include our romantic partner – husband or wife – and our children. Our romantic partner is probably our primary relationship, but if we have children they are extremely important to us too, taking enormous amounts of our time and attention, ideally in co-operation with our romantic partner. And in this typical picture we will have another circle which contains less close family members. And another which includes close friends. And another which includes less close friends and colleagues. And so on. And there will also be a kind of outer circle for people who serve specific roles in our lives, for example, our doctor, shop assistants, restaurant waiters and so forth. We may not be close to these people but we need to know how to relate to them in an appropriate way. And how we relate to people in our inner circle will usually be somewhat different to how we relate to people in our outer circle.

Even though all these stages of social development are very complex, they usually happen quite naturally. But Asperger Syndrome is a hidden disability; when you have AS, many of these natural processes do not happen so readily. This is a real impairment and it can have a profound impact on your life, but it is hard for other people to really understand. Allowances are often not made, and it is hard for you to get the help that you need and deserve.

Relationships with other people are extremely important. They affect the quality of life in many significant ways. When relationships go well, life can be like heaven. But none of us goes through life without experiencing loneliness at times, so we know the pain of being disappointed and unsuccessful in our relationships. And at times like these, life can be hell.

As parents, one of the most important – and most difficult – services which we can perform for our children is to help them learn to relate to other people. The task is very important because what we are really trying to do is to set them up for life in such a way that their future relationships can be happy and successful. And the Social Curriculum which teaches these things is unfortunately not given the priority it deserves in schools.

225 It's the hardest subject of all

The Social Curriculum is arguably the hardest subject of all – to teach and to learn – for several reasons. It is, of course, a very complex curriculum, yet most people learn relationship and social skills quite naturally and do not need too much specific teaching. Generally the learning process happens gradually as we grow up, so that we do not even realise we are learning it – it is not really a conscious kind of learning. But people with AS find it hard to learn the Social Curriculum and they may have to learn much of it in a very conscious way – and that in itself makes it very difficult.

Think about how difficult it is to learn to do a task which you do not know innately how to do. You have to think of every step consciously.

Take driving a car, for example. When you are learning to drive you think very consciously about everything you are doing. Each step is broken down into manageable chunks, clearly explained to you, repeated and reinforced. It takes a lot of time and repetition before you perform each step quite automatically. Eventually you do not have to think each time you get in to the car 'Now I must take off the handbrake and look in the mirror and signal my intentions', and so on. You just do it. You don't have to think because it has become automatic to you. Finally, instead of thinking consciously about the process of driving you can think about your journey.

Learning the Social Curriculum is of course immensely more difficult than learning to drive a car, and people are far more complex and less predictable than machines, especially when they are swayed by their emotions. And it is also far more difficult to teach the Social Curriculum, because anything that we do automatically can be hard to teach.

Take a simple example – tying your shoe laces. How do you do it? It is hard to explain because you do it so automatically. If you had to write out a set of absolutely clear and unambiguous instructions, breaking the task down into manageable steps so they could be understood by someone who had no idea how to do it, how do you think you would manage? Perhaps you can have a go and see how hard it is to break down and explain even this most simple task. And it is infinitely more difficult and complex to break down social rules and conventions so as to teach the Social Curriculum.

Our job in teaching the Social Curriculum to our children is no mean task. We need to see it as a very long-term project and we need just about infinite patience.

226 To learn is to grow

It is good to be real with your child about the social difficulties associated with Asperger Syndrome and the problems these difficulties can cause. But balance this by reassuring him that you will help him to learn the Social Curriculum and encouraging him to have an attitude of resolve, determination and self-confidence. Foster a positive attitude to learning – that learning can make life worthwhile and interesting – and, by words and example, help see himself as capable of change and learning.

227 Help him understand the social game

A young person with AS can end up feeling like a failure and inadequate because he is not skilful socially. Help him to realise that whether he is socially skilful or not, this is not an issue of personal worth, value or morality. Help him see that the social world is like a kind of game with rules that some people know better than others, and that people with AS usually do not know the rules very well – that is part of Aspergers.

Social skills are important, yes, and learning them will hopefully make your path through life easier, but in themselves they will not make you a better person. Some people who are very charming and socially successful are hypocritical and mean, and some people who are shy, gauche and awkward are heroic and cool.

Ultimately it is up to him whether he wants to play the game and, if so, to what extent. But help him see that learning to play the game may give him an advantage in life. Even if he does not like the game, there is no harm in him learning something about it and knowing at least some of the rules – if only for interest!

The basic questions you will need to answer for him are:

- What's the point?

- How does it work?

- What am I missing?

See the tips below for further ideas.

228 There's more than one right answer

Emphasise to your child that the Social Curriculum is not an exact science. It is more like a series of guidelines and observations about how things normally work. Because, in reality, much social behaviour involves mirroring the behaviour of other people and being careful not to step on their toes.

When it comes to 'getting things right' in social situations there are usually many wrong answers. But there are guidelines, and there can be many right answers as well.

229 Help him see the point

Your child may not see the point in learning the social rules. Or he may have rationalised things so he doesn't care about other people and how he relates to them. But there are some advantages which you can explain to him logically, and you can help him see the benefits by pointing out for example that:

- *Other people can help us get to know ourselves.* We can get to know aspects of ourselves by means of our relationships with other people, and there are many advantages to self-awareness (see also Tip 265).

- *It pays to be nice.* When you are nice to people they are more likely to be nice to you!

- *Teamwork has its plus sides.* When a group of people co-operate and pool their resources they can often achieve a better result.

- *Diplomacy can be a good idea.* When you make people feel good about themselves they are more likely to be nice to you.

- *Disrespect closes ears.* When you talk to people in a way that is respectful their ears open up.

- *Being mean is often counter-productive.* When you are hard on other people you usually make things hard for yourself as well.

230 It's like learning to swim

Teaching your child the Social Curriculum is a bit like teaching a child to swim when he has some kind of water phobia. If you think about it this way, it can be a helpful analogy. First you need to realise and accept that your child has some kind of phobia, aversion, fear or at least dislike of the water (i.e. social interaction), for whatever reason. He is far from being a natural swimmer and it is never going to work for you to simply throw him in at the deep end.

This is not a question of 'sink or swim'. If you just throw him in he will probably sink. Even if you manage to rescue him, he may be so traumatised that he will be very reluctant to go near the water again. (In other words, he may hide in his room and not come out.)

If someone does not know how to swim he needs to be taught by someone who does – and the buck probably falls with you. Even if you are not a great swimmer yourself, the chances are that you are better than him.

Just like the example of shoelace tying (see also Tip 225) you will need to analyse something you normally do automatically before you can pass it on. This is a big, complex job; it is extremely difficult, and it will take an enormous amount of time and patience. But it may be the only way your child is ever going to learn to swim, and it could hardly be more important. This is part of the work of real love.

Translating the analogy into real life a bit more, you may need to start off by setting up social situations which you know he can manage, and build from there very slowly. For example:

- Involve him in the planning and make it enjoyable.

- Do something social which you know he will be comfortable with – nothing too demanding.

- It may be best to avoid situations which involve too many people or where there is too much hurly burly going on.

- Start one to one. Gradually perhaps include another person, and then another.

- Err on the side of making the social occasion a short but positive one.

- Don't try to teach him specific social skills when he is in a social situation which is stressing him out. The timing needs to be right. There is no point in trying to teach a drowning man to swim.

231 Break it down

You know how to swim, at least to a small extent. You can pass this on to him, but because he may not learn much simply from watching and copying, a big part of your job is to figure out what exactly it is you are doing, break it into manageable steps and pass it on to him. How are you managing to keep afloat and make it from one side of the pool to the other? What are the social skills that most people just know and he doesn't? Ideally, by words, practice and example, you can help him learn about all the main components of relationships. For example:

- *Starting*. Help him see the point of introductory pleasantries and small talk when you first meet someone: They can help things run more smoothly and put people at their ease.

- *Maintaining*. Like many things in life, relationships need maintenance. This can take the form of the odd phone call, for example, answering texts, spending time together and so on.

- *Fine tuning*. Over time relationships change and slight adaptations may be made to suit those concerned.

- *Repair*. It is normal for things to go wrong between people sometimes, because no one is perfect. When this happens you may need to address certain issues. There may need to be negotiations, apologies and forgiveness before you move on. Sometimes when relationships go through these things and are handled well, they move on from strength to strength.

- *Ending*. It is important to know how and when to consider ending a relationship. Sometimes it is not your choice. Someone may end a relationship with you and it is possible that you may be hurt when this happens. Sometimes perhaps it is your choice. You want to move on and do not want to be involved anymore with another person. If so, someone else may get hurt. It is your right to end a relationship of course, but you should try to handle it well – with honesty and respect. You will feel better about yourself if you do.

232 Analyse social behaviour

To teach your child the Social Curriculum you will need to develop a completely new analytical mental habit. You will need to look carefully at your own social behaviour and the social behaviour of others and figure out what is going on. What unwritten rules are in play, what works well and what not so well?

So in some ways we need to teach ourselves the Social Curriculum before we can pass it on to our children. Again, this is a very long-term task.

233 Start in the shallow pool

As well as learning the rules, your child will need to practise them in order to gain confidence and improve. In other words, over time you will need to find ways to entice him out of his room to engage with the world.

If a child had an extreme aversion to water, his only hope of learning to swim might be to go to the pool with his instructor when it is quiet and empty. He might need time to get used to the feel of the water, and he might do better if he practises in the shallow pool at first. This might need to be repeated many times so he can get used to the experience. In the end he might even start to enjoy it – for there is something unspeakably rewarding about overcoming a deep fear or phobia, and for young people with AS, social situations can be a bit like that.

234 Approach it like coaching sessions

Using the learning to swim analogy again, the job of the coach includes teaching and instructing. During lessons and practice sessions a good coach makes careful observations so that he can give helpful feedback to encourage progress as well as constructive feedback to suggest improvement.

It is important for the pupil to trust his swimming coach so that he takes the feedback in the spirit it is intended: to help him do better. You can equip your child to deal with social situations by teaching him some of the strategies suggested in Tips 235–40.

235 Reflect and rehearse

In advance of some social situations it can be useful to help your child to think ahead about the detail and imagine what it will be like:

- Where are you going?
- What time does it start and end?
- Have you been there before?
- What will it be like?
- Who else will be there?
- What will be going on?
- Do you need to arrange transport?

Think and plan ahead so you have some idea in your head about how to greet people, make small talk, keep the conversation going, take an interest in others, listen, give appropriate compliments and so on.

If there is some specific situation that he is concerned about, perhaps some kind of role play might be helpful? And after social events, obviously choosing your moment and without seeming to pry, encourage reflection:

- How did it go?

- What went well?

- Were there any problems and if so how might they be prevented next time?

236 Try using scripts

It can be difficult to think of what to say in difficult situations in the spur of the moment. What difficult situations is your child likely to encounter? Help him to think about them in advance and have a couple of 'rescue phrases' to hand. Rescue phrases should be short, easily memorable phrases designed to deal with specific situations.

To take a simple example, say your child has been invited to some kind social event. He is not sure if he will enjoy it and would like to try it without being pressurised to come back the following week. If he is questioned or coaxed in this situation, rescue phrases might include:

'I'm not sure what my plans are yet.'

'I will phone you if I am planning to come again.'

Or even:

'To be honest, I don't think it's really for me. But thanks for inviting me anyway.'

Help him understand some of the following unwritten 'rules' of social dynamics (Tips 237–240).

237 It's the thought that counts

In general people enjoy receiving gifts. It is great, of course, to give a gift of an item that the recipient actually wants and would have chosen for himself – but sometimes just a small gift or card can serve as a gesture of care, friendship and so on.

238 Use compliments

People enjoy receiving compliments. Your child doesn't need to give insincere compliments, of course, but if he finds something in another person that is worth complimenting, they will like the fact that he noticed.

239 Help him make amends

When your child gets it wrong, help him to admit it, apologise, make amends and ask himself, 'What could I do differently next time?'

240 Great conversationalists can be very quiet

Most people enjoy talking about themselves. So your child doesn't actually need to be a great conversationalist. If you help him to develop the knack of asking someone a few key questions, let them talk about themselves, and listen to what they say, it is surprising how often that person will come away with a good impression of your child's social skills. He may not have said much, but his conversation partner has appreciated talking about himself so much that he genuinely believes your child is an interesting person and great company!

EMOTIONS AND NONVERBAL COMMUNICATION

TIP BOX

Emotions and nonverbal communication

241 It's like a foreign language to Aspies

242 Help him fill in the gaps

243 Explain social masks

244 Translate intentions

245 Verbalise the rules

246 Mute it

247 Help him understand that hierarchies matter

248 Understand emotions in context

249 Name feelings

250 'It's not unusual'

251 You're not the only one

252 Spell out the impact

253 Understand responsibility versus guilt

254 It's good to talk

255 Solitude can help

241 It's like a foreign language to Aspies

In general what is termed 'social communication' is the most difficult form of communication for people with AS. Why? Presumably because usually when people are together, much of what goes on consists of nonverbal communication. In fact it is said that over 90 per cent of interpersonal communication is nonverbal, and yet for a person with AS this form of communication can be a bit like a foreign language. This is a well-known difficulty for people with AS, and the subtleties and complexities of nonverbal communication can be an absolute minefield during adolescence.

So it's easy to see why adolescent Aspies are much more at home in front of a computer screen, and why they may usually be happy to spend unbelievable lengths of time communicating with their online friends, yet very reluctant to step outside the bubble of their own bedroom to do so in the 'real world'. Many adolescents are like this of course, but the situation is often much more extreme for an adolescent with Asperger Syndrome.

242 Help him fill in the gaps

It is usually a mistake to assume that your child picks up on nonverbal clues and pointers. Unless things are spelled out – in words – very clearly, there is a good chance that 'the obvious' will escape him, and he may be completely oblivious of hints and nuances.

You can do a lot to help to fill in the gaps in his social awareness by drawing his attention to the nonverbal information that he is missing, in a calm, clear, matter-of-fact way. But first you may need to make a great effort to figure out what the nonverbal 'subtext' is. This is not always easy but, where appropriate, you could consider talking to him with the aim of helping him understand about social masks, translating the intentions of others and telling him the nonverbal rules.

243 Explain social masks

Help your child understand that most people wear what is known as a 'social mask'. In other words, they present to the world slightly different versions of themselves depending on the circumstances. These differences may be quite innocent and benign. For example, most people behave in a more polite way in company and feel they can relax their standards when they are within the four walls of their home. But at the most sinister end of the continuum there are people in the world who are deliberately and maliciously two-faced and hypocritical.

Thankfully such people are rare, but between these two extremes there is a whole range of variations. So it is well advised not to jump to conclusions about people too quickly. It is wiser to suspend judgement and make an assessment of their personality and trustworthiness based on how they behave and treat other people over a period of time.

244 Translate intentions

Because people wear social masks it can be a mistake to always take what they say at absolute face value. Unless your child properly understands this, he can be very vulnerable, so you may need to be discreetly vigilant about what is going on in his life and who he is associating with.

Be cautious about interfering, of course, but if you believe he is in danger of being exploited or bullied, you may need to translate the intentions of people who mean him harm, and guide him away from dangerous or inappropriate situations.

245 Verbalise the rules

When people get together there are always unwritten and unspoken rules. They are assumed and taken for granted. In general people do not think or talk about them. The only time they are really aware of them is when someone breaks them. The problem for the young person with AS is that he may fall into the trap of breaking rules that he has no awareness of. He does not even know they exist. All he may know is that sometimes for no apparent reason people seem to prefer to avoid him, but they don't tell him why.

In principle it is very unfair to punish anyone for breaking rules when he doesn't even know they exist –

especially when these rules are usually, in the greater scheme of things, unimportant. For the rules that Aspies break have usually nothing to do with morality. In reality social rules are often little more than convention.

Since no one else is likely to tell your child the social rules, it may end up being your job. As usual you will have your own background work to do in order to figure out what the relevant rules actually are. To take a simple example, if he has rubbed people up the wrong way in company, you can observe, use your judgement and try to figure out where he might be going wrong. If and when it is appropriate tell him the rules in words. To take a simple example you might say – when the moment is right of course: 'As far as I can see, each of your friends take turns at paying for petrol when you go out. I get the feeling it might be some kind of unspoken rule.'

246 Mute it

Body language is another form of nonverbal communication which your child may be blind to. This is also hard to teach, but there are resources available that can be helpful (try the 'Body Language' section from the Improve Your Social Skills website – see the Useful Websites section for details). One idea which can be fun is to watch some kind of drama or comedy with the sound on mute and see if you can figure out what is going on and how people are feeling from their nonverbal communication – facial expression, gestures and so on (Nierenberg and Calero 1980).

247 Help him understand that hierarchies matter

Teach your child in words about the concept of authority. He may not agree with it or like it but it can do no harm for him to at least get the principle that there are various hierarchies among people and in society. Some are more obvious than others, for example most people defer to other people when they perceive them as figures of authority,

248 Understand emotions in context

Especially at this age, some Aspies can experience extremes of emotions which they find it hard to understand or manage. Rage can become a problem, for example, when your child is set up by others, and it is always worth maintaining an attitude of vigilance to minimise the chance of him finding himself at the mercy of predators (Attwood 2013).

You may remember your own adolescence, when sometimes your emotions ran high. You may have been sure that no one in the world had ever felt the way you do. If your child ever feels like that it can help to remind him of the simple truth – that time heals all ills, and that this painful time will pass and not last forever.

Even weather and time-related analogies, which might otherwise seem like clichés, can be helpful as long as they come from a sincere heart. For example:

- Even on a lovely bright day, it only takes one cloud to block out the sun, but clouds pass and weather changes.

- There will always be sunny days and stormy days, but they never last forever.

- Tomorrow is another day full of mystery and hope.

249 Name feelings

Try not to worry too much or show any overreaction when you see you child going through the extreme kind of emotions that are sometimes called teenage angst. In general a calm, logical approach can help and there can be something reassuring when you can at least put a name to an emotion.

Try to encourage open, matter-of-fact communication about emotions. As always be sensitive, don't force things, and choose your timing. Guide the conversation in such a way as to name as accurately as you can whatever feeling you think he is feeling. For example you might say in a calm but concerned tone 'When that happened you must have been very upset' (or anxious, or worried, or devastated, or whatever you assess to be close to what he is feeling).

There is a chance that in response he might disagree completely with your assessment. I remember doing this with my son once and he contradicted every adjective I had suggested. 'Not really, I was just apprehensive,' he told me in the end! But that is OK. It is actually better if he comes up with own adjectives and names his own emotions.

And if he denies that he was feeling anything at all, and that he 'doesn't care', that is fine too. It is best then to let the matter drop. You have at least planted a seed.

250 'It's not unusual'

In the course of any discussions with your child about his feelings, try to help him understand and accept that extreme emotions are normal, especially at his age, when hormones play such a part. And that, even though it may be confusing, it is perfectly normal for him to experience two contradictory feelings at the same time.

251 You're not the only one

Nobody finds it easy to think about or consider other people when they are upset, so this is a conversation that should happen ideally at a moment when your child is in good form and you know he is receptive, not when he is under pressure and immersed in his own emotions.

Make sure he knows that other people have emotions too and that everyone's emotions deserve respect.

252 Spell out the impact

If you can help your child to see the perspective of another person, things can begin to change. Make it a goal to help him think through the impact of his choices and behaviour and put himself in the shoes of the other person and imagine how he might feel. This will need to be done as a conscious mental exercise and of course the timing needs to be right for such a conversation.

253 Understand responsibility versus guilt

Yes, your child may lack empathy sometimes. It is part of the condition of Asperger Syndrome, and as a result he may do things which seem thoughtless and rub people up the wrong way.

When this happens you can help him see the impact of his choices. But be careful that you do not put a 'guilt trip' on to him. Guilt inducing is generally not a wise or effective motivator. We know the difference between guilt and responsibility. We just need to keep it in mind.

Nobody enjoys feeling guilty. Guilt makes you feel bad about yourself and it is tempting to slip into denial rather than face guilt. Responsibility, on the other hand, is about facing consequences with an attitude of something closer to curiosity and learning. Aim to encourage your child to take responsibility rather than feel guilty.

254 It's good to talk

It really is good to talk sometimes, and you can be a listening ear for your child. Encourage him to talk about his emotions to you or other trusted adults or even to a properly trained professional if you feel he needs to. But at the same time keep a balance. Talking too much can lead to obsession and make things worse sometimes. You are the best person to gauge when your child needs to talk and when it is better to suggest a limit. At such times advise him on the wisdom of stopping talking about his problems for a specified time. They will still be there when he goes back, and he might see them from a fresh perspective.

255 Solitude can help

It is common for young people with AS to spend long periods alone in their bedroom. In fact it is a common phenomenon, even without Asperger Syndrome, for young people to need a lot of space. But if you are concerned that he is becoming too isolated, try to agree with him a specified time limit for his solitude.

He may need times of solitude to allow him to process his emotions, but as usual it is wise to keep an eye on things to make sure they do not get out of balance.

POSITIVE SOCIAL EXPERIENCES

TIP BOX

Positive social experiences

256 Time alone – whose problem is it?

257 Agree limits on solitary activities

258 One man's meat is another man's poison

259 Be selective

260 Think of alternatives to small talk

261 Discuss romantic and sexual relationships?

262 Realise that online relationships matter

263 Challenge your attitude

264 Be careful with the internet

256 Time alone – whose problem is it?

Keep an eye on your child and watch out for signs of depression, but do not be overly concerned if your child spends long periods alone. People with AS do genuinely prefer and need to be alone sometimes. And sometimes parents project their own feelings about this and worry needlessly.

If your child is genuinely happy and his alone time is not too out of balance, ask yourself how much of a problem it really is. Don't forget – plenty of other young people spend a lot of time socialising at night clubs and so on, and their parents worry constantly about their safety. Those parents would probably envy your problem!

257 Agree limits on solitary activities

If he needs time alone, accept it, but encourage him to limit it in advance. Tell him for example that a lazy day in his room is fine now and then, but that if it develops into day after day where he does not get dressed or come out of his room, you are concerned that he might end up getting isolated and depressed. If you talk to him in advance at the right moment, hopefully he will see the sense of this and agree. Assuming he does, ask for his suggestions as to how you can help if you see things slipping out of balance in the future. He might suggest something zany and effective, for example, that as you come into his room, you should leave windows and doors open and play his least favourite music loudly. Approaches like this can work if they are carried out in a calm, good-humoured way – especially if they were originally his suggestion!

258 One man's meat is another man's poison

It can be very tempting to project on to our children our own ideas about what they should and shouldn't like or enjoy socially. And often this is based on our own faded memories of what we liked and enjoyed when we were his age.

For example, perhaps your school formal or prom stands out fondly in your recollections when you look back on your teenage years. In your mind you have categorised it as a special event. And maybe you can't help looking forward to watching your child's enjoyment when he reaches that milestone himself. You imagine you will be able to relive your own happy memories, and that you will be very proud of him!

However, you may need to make a conscious effort to step into your child's shoes and see things from his point of view. If he is showing no interest, it may be because events like this are not important to him and he does not see the point of them. Or it may be that he hates the very thought of it – so much that he does not even want to talk about it. One way or another, it really is his life. And sometimes the things that are a source of delight and pleasure to typical teens and young adults are a source of dread and anticipation to young people with Asperger Syndrome. That's just how it is and you may need to accept it.

If you hate the thought of your child missing out on some kind of special event, why not talk to him about it openly? Tell him how you feel, that you understand and accept that he is not like most kids his age in many ways, and that he has his own ideas and tastes. But you would like it if you could think of something that he would actually enjoy instead. Perhaps you could have a family meeting and come up with some kind of 'prom alternative' to look forward to.

259 Be selective

As a rule of thumb, it is better to err on the side of fewer successful social events, than many unsuccessful social events. The last thing you want to do is reinforce your child's aversion to socialising and any self-concept he may have as an unsociable or socially unsuccessful person.

Encourage him to socialise only when you feel the circumstances are right, and when you have reason to believe it will be a socially successful experience for him. He needs to be selective about where he goes and who he is with. Keep an eye on who he is associating with, and do what you can to encourage people you trust to be involved in his life. He may or may not enjoy being with other young people with AS, and socialising with other Aspies may be worth exploring. You might be able to find organised groups of young people with Asperger Syndrome (National Autistic Society 2013c).

260 Think of alternatives to small talk

To break the ice at a get-together, games, puzzles and quizzes can be much easier than small talk for a young person with AS, particularly interactive games such as board games or playing cards. But something like Sudoko can be fun for a few people to work on together.

261 Discuss romantic and sexual relationships?

Most young people like to keep their private lives private. At least from their parents! So it is probably important to your child to know that certain taboos will be respected, and you need to be sensitive to this. Romantic relationships and sex are very likely to fall into this category, whether your child has Asperger Syndrome or not. His dignity, pride and self-respect may be at stake here, so it is important that we respect the taboos.

On the other hand, we know more about these things than he thinks we do – just as our parents did before us. And we can see round corners that he cannot see – again just as our parents before us. For in these areas there really is nothing new under the sun.

There are certain dangers that we naturally want to protect our child from, and we know we have sound advice to offer. But how do we deliver that protection and advice while still respecting our child's dignity? There are certain things we can do to (1) ensure he is aware of the 'facts of life' and (2) encourage a responsible attitude to sex (see also Tip 271).

262 Realise that online relationships matter

Quite often parents don't take their children's online relationships very seriously. We tend to think of them as second best, especially if the relationships are with people at the other end of the world, so that there is little prospect of them ever meeting each other. But perhaps we need to stop and think. What constitutes a relationship anyway?

Unless you grew up in the age of the internet yourself it is hard to imagine how important this has become as a means of communication for young people. And for young people with Asperger Syndrome the internet can be especially important. So accept the importance of online relationships and don't belittle them. They may matter to your child more than you realise and they can serve an important role (see also Tip 28).

263 Challenge your attitude

There are many advantages to the idea of connecting with people via the internet. An obvious one for Aspies is that they have a chance which they would not otherwise have to exchange ideas with like-minded people.

If a young person with AS feels misunderstood and really struggles to find anyone on his wavelength, it can be a wonderful thing for him to find an online friend whom he can relate to. The exchange of ideas may be more important to him than we can understand, and the dialogue that can flow from such connections can be very interesting and valuable to him too.

So, if you have a cynical attitude about online relationships, challenge your own prejudices. The world is changing all the time. Who is to say that online relationships are inferior or not real?

264 Be careful with the internet

Obviously there are dangers with the internet. One concern is that too much time in front of a screen can keep your child from 'real life' and so it can be useful to negotiate limits. But in this respect young people with

AS are probably not that different to most young people these days.

Another concern is that the internet brings with it the risk of corruption, bad influences, pornography, violence and the like. And, again, young people with AS are not in an unusual position.

When it comes to the internet, always take sensible precautions to protect your child and make him aware of online dangers.

10

Preparation for Adulthood

Encouraging self-awareness and responsibility
Thinking about college and career
Encouraging a positive outlook

Help prepare and equip your child for adulthood by:

- Encouraging self-awareness and responsibility (page 182)

- Thinking about college and career (page 189)

- Encouraging a positive outlook (page 194)

ENCOURAGING SELF-AWARENESS AND RESPONSIBILITY

TIP BOX

Encouraging self-awareness and responsibility

265 Show him how to 'know thyself'
266 Encourage his self-awareness and maturity
267 Understand that mirrors are voluntary
268 Build his Asperger awareness
269 Give him his say
270 Recognise his profile of extremes
271 Discuss the 'facts of life'
272 Talk about romance and primary relationships?

265 Show him how to 'know thyself'

Aim to equip your child with a healthy self-awareness. In an ideal scenario, he will make self-awareness his own personal mission, which, rather than impose upon him, you can help him with. To this end, help him see the point of the Ancient Greek wisdom which counsels 'know thyself'.

Do what you can to present self-awareness to him as an interesting journey and an intelligent goal. You can do this by means of discussion, debate and, most importantly, by example – he will be more likely to adopt self-awareness as a goal when he sees you consciously adopt and benefit from it as a goal in your own life.

266 Encourage his self-awareness and maturity

Help your child understand that:

- Self-awareness is a vital tool which can lead to maturity and self-mastery.

- All your behaviour and choices have consequences to some extent.

- Self-awareness includes becoming aware of the impact of your behaviour and choices on other people.

- It is wise to weigh up the likely impact of your behaviour and choices.

- Some of your choices and decisions, especially as you approach adulthood, can have an impact on your life and the lives of other people for a long time to come.

- Adult responsibility always involves taking into consideration the impact of your choices and behaviour – especially if the impact may be long term or extreme.

267 Understand that mirrors are voluntary

Encouraging self-awareness in your child is, of course, a very long-term process, for in reality it is a life-long task for any of us. And it needs to be handled with great humility and sensitivity.

Many people go through life blissfully unaware of aspects of themselves which other people can see easily, and they have little interest in being made aware of how other people see them (unless of course this takes the form of flattery!).

But it is sometimes helpful to hold a mirror up to the people we love (see Tip 165) because it can help them see more realistically some things about themselves which they might otherwise never see. And seeing these things can put them at an advantage insofar as it can help them manage their lives better.

Holding up a mirror to other people in this way can actually be part of love, but only when done in the right way and for the right reasons – between people who love and trust each other and who have some kind of understanding that it is being done with the conscious aim of mutual self-improvement.

268 Build his Asperger awareness

Your child is a unique individual of whom Asperger Syndrome is a part. Understanding Asperger Syndrome and the part it plays in his life can put him at an advantage for the rest of his life. Aim to make him 'Asperger aware'.

Refer to the Seven Key Insights section of this book (Chapter 3) and some of the earlier tips in the book which were specifically aimed at encouraging self-awareness:

1. Asperger extremes (Tips 19–23)
2. Fish out of water (Tips 24–34)
3. Rates of development (Tips 35–43)
4. Processing and sensory differences (Tips 44–52)
5. Mind blindness (Tips 53–64)
6. Rigidity (Tips 65–73)
7. Social vulnerability (Tips 74–85)

269 Give him his say

Listen to your child's opinion. Adolescence can be the age of contempt, so it is possible that he may scoff or sneer at any insights you have to offer. If he does, that's OK. It's probably even healthy. But there is no point in forcing things any further at least for now. Seeds have been planted at least.

He may also have his own alternative slant on Asperger Syndrome which he thinks is superior. And that's fine too.

Listen to what he has to say. His ideas may be fascinating and original and you may have something to learn from them. Any debate that follows may help you understand and connect with each other better.

270 Recognise his profile of extremes

When you get to grips with the idea that Asperger Syndrome is all about extremes and opposites, it can be a real key to understanding and self-awareness.

Keep in mind – your child will have his or her own unique profile which may comprise a wide and complex range of extremes.

271 Discuss the 'facts of life'

It is common for there to be certain taboos between parents and children, especially around the age of adolescence. This is completely natural and there is usually little point in trying to force discussions in areas where either you or your child feels unhappy or uncomfortable. A common taboo area is, of course, sex and, in reality, most young people have little interest in what their parents have to say about sex and romance – especially during adolescence. However, the following principles may be helpful:

- *The right age?* Make sure your child is aware of the 'facts of life' at an appropriate age. As a rule of thumb, earlier is better than later. It is easier to talk about these things at a point *before* he can personally relate to them, ideally before hormones have set in. That means that by the time of adolescence he should already be in the picture.

- *The best source.* These days very few children are 'innocent' about sexual matters. They can learn them very easily from friends, TV, school, the internet and so on. But the facts of life are best learned within the family where you have control over how they are presented and can answer questions accurately.

- *The right information.* As well as the basic facts of life make sure he is fully informed about contraception and sexually transmitted diseases.

- *The right attitude.* Put him in the picture in a matter-of-fact, unemotional but respectful way. Emphasise that sexual activity should be part of an otherwise intimate relationship, and that it involves responsibility and can have real and long-term consequences.

- *Values and standards.* Encourage him to have a responsible and moral attitude about sex and caution him against recklessness and impulsivity.

- *Open to questions.* Answer questions as accurately as you can, without making him feel stupid or embarrassed. At the same time you may want to urge him to be discreet by explaining that talking about sexual matters is inappropriate in many settings.

- *Resources.* Unless you are a biology teacher, you may not feel equipped to explain the facts of life properly or to answer questions. If so consider letting him read an appropriate book or watch a video that will give him all the information he needs. Obviously choose the resources carefully.

Ideally, watch the video together with him rather than letting him watch it on his own.

272 Talk about romance and primary relationships?

There is usually only a certain amount of input that a young person wants to hear from their parents about romantic relationships. Understandably young people generally regard this area as a private one, and boundaries need to be respected.

You may have good solid advice to pass on to him, but it may be hard to find the opportunity. There is no point in trying to force discussions about romantic relationships. Just be there for when the right moment arises and be receptive if he wants to talk to you. In general the advice you want to pass on to him is:

- When you have Asperger Syndrome romantic relationships can be more difficult and complicated.

- Most people play the 'dating game' whereby they spend time with potential partners, usually one to one. Sometimes dates lead to longer-term relationships and even marriage, sometimes not.

- People with AS are often not very good at the dating game, because there are a lot of unwritten rules.

- You may or may not want to get involved in the dating game. If you do, it is best for you to just be yourself. That way you will attract the kind of partner who accepts you for who you are.

- When it comes to dating it is helpful if you know as much as you can about the Social Curriculum.

- When you feel good about yourself you are more likely to attract the right partner.

- Primary romantic relationships are not for everyone. In the end what matters is that you find happiness in life and feel good about yourself, whether you have a romantic partner or not.

- A good relationship is worth waiting for.

- In a good relationship each person feels free to be themselves and they bring out the best in each other.

- The right partner understands and respects you for who you are.

- In reality it can be harder to find a good relationship when you have Asperger Syndrome, but the right partner is worth waiting for.

THINKING ABOUT COLLEGE AND CAREER

TIP BOX

Thinking about college and career

273   Consider continuing education?
274   Notify future employers and educators?
275   Identify levels of support
276   Find extra assistance
277   Get off on the right foot
278   Establish agreed contact times
279   Be vigilant

273 Consider continuing education?

Unfortunately for many people with Asperger Syndrome, school can be a challenging and unhappy time, and during adolescence there are new decisions to be made. Should your child stay in education beyond the age of compulsory education? If so, what are the best options for further education? Or should he try to get a job instead?

Here are a few of the considerations to keep in mind:

- If he does not enjoy school, the idea of continuing education for its own sake may seem pointless to him. If he has a clear idea about what he would like to do in terms of career, help him establish very specifically what the requirements are, and make plans accordingly.

- He may, for example, need certain academic qualifications to help him move towards where he wants to go. If so he is more likely to see a clear purpose in continuing education and to be more motivated and co-operative.

- If his career choice is not an academic one and he is having a hard time at school, there is probably little point in pressurising him to continue his academic education. Look into other career routes: training colleges, apprenticeships and so on. Or help him to find a job which he will enjoy and which will help him feel successful.

- If education has been miserable for him up till now, consider a year or so out of school. Many young people take gap years after school so this is not necessarily such an unusual idea.

- It is better to have at least some kind of purpose or idea in mind for a gap year rather than leaving it completely aimless – even a simple purpose such as getting into shape mentally and physically can be a good starting point.

- A gap year might be beneficial as a kind of 'mental health break' during which you can help your child to explore different options and think carefully about his next step.

274 Notify future employers and educators?

Is it a good idea for future employers and educators to be notified about your child's Asperger diagnosis? A lot depends on his point of view. On one hand, your child may want the opportunity to make a fresh start, and find out how he manages in a new situation where people do not have any preconceptions about him. On the other hand, it is unrealistic to expect people to provide support and make due allowances if they are kept in the dark!

You may need to talk through the pros and cons with him carefully. It is possible that you may have a more realistic idea than him about the level of support he needs and the new challenges he is likely to face. Weigh it up carefully, but overall there is probably a stronger argument in favour of notifying future employers and educators than not.

275 Identify levels of support

When helping your child to choose a suitable job, college or university, try to establish as clearly as possible what level of support he is likely to receive. Look for an establishment which has a good reputation for understanding and supporting people with AS.

- Research thoroughly what options are available.

- Make contact with support staff.

- Discuss your child's specific profile and needs.

- Ask around.

- Speak to other students or parents who have firsthand experience.

276 Find extra assistance

Colleges and universities will generally have dealt with many students with Asperger Syndrome, so they should have their own support structure that your child can tap into. Get as much information as you can on what support is available and how it might be of use. It can be a great help if, for example:

- he is assigned an individual support assistant or mentor

- he is granted an extra time allowance for exams and assignments

- he gets permission to sit his exams in some location other than the exam hall – perhaps under the supervision of an exam supervisor in a specified separate room.

On the other hand prospective employers, especially smaller employers, may not have so much experience of Asperger Syndrome. If so, they may be glad of specific suggestions as to how they can help.

There may be even small steps which they can take which will go a long way to make life easier for a person with Asperger Syndrome, for example:

- providing him with important information in clear written form

- assigning an appropriate person to him as a kind of ally or mentor

- nominating a specified retreat area where your child can, when necessary, spend short agreed periods of time.

277 Get off on the right foot

It will serve you and your child well if he and you can establish good, co-operative relationships from the word go with the people who will be dealing with him on an ongoing basis: teachers, employers, support staff and so on. Help your child to see the point of this and encourage him to put his best foot forward, so to speak, at initial meetings and interviews. These people will want things to run smoothly and successfully just as much as you do.

It will take new people time to get to know your child and it is hard for them to really know what to expect initially – what problems to anticipate and how they can best provide your child with the support he needs.

Even if they have access to written reports from previous educators and so on, it can be very helpful for them to talk directly to you and your child about relevant issues. Ideally they will see you as a useful point of contact – approachable and easy to get along with, available to help if necessary further down the line – and not as some kind of interference!

278 Establish agreed contact times

If your child has been assigned a support assistant or mentor, it is unrealistic to expect this person to be available 24/7. Suggest that agreed contact times are arranged when your child can check in with this person if he needs to and vice versa.

279 Be vigilant

Keep an eye on who your child is associating with and – without being paranoid of course – be vigilant for signs of bullying (see also Tip 80).

ENCOURAGING A POSITIVE OUTLOOK

TIP BOX

Encouraging a positive outlook

280 It's a matter of choice
281 Encourage positivity
282 'Always look on the bright side'
283 Acknowledge problems
284 Focus on solutions
285 Find out about inspirational role models
286 Remember that worrying is useless

See also Tips 141–56.

280 It's a matter of choice

Most people would agree, I'm sure, that it is a good idea to try to adopt a positive outlook on life. But it is not surprising that people with AS are sometimes negative, given the difficulties that they face on a daily basis.

Encourage your child to see the benefits of a positive outlook on life and help him to realise that positivity is a conscious, healthy and intelligent choice. Help him see, for example:

- When you are aware of both the pluses and the minuses in a given situation, you can then choose what to focus on.

- A glass which is half empty is also half full. Both are true. It just depends how you look at it!

- The most mature and intelligent attitude to life is to focus on the positives while simultaneously finding ways to manage, deal with and learn from the negatives.

281 Encourage positivity

Foster in and around him an attitude of positivity by example, encouragement and inspiration.

Encourage a positive attitude to him as an individual (see also Tips 141–7) and a positive attitude to AS (see also Tips 148–56).

282 'Always look on the bright side'

Give him some light hearted things to think about:

- Life can be an interesting, fun journey.

- If you really put your mind to it, you can always find some changes which you can make, to improve a situation.

- It is always possible to find a win-win way forward if you try hard enough.

- Lighten up and remind him of the Monty Python song! 'Always look on the bright side of life...'

283 Acknowledge problems

Life is full of problems. We cannot escape them. The only issue is how we deal with them. When problems come along it can be tempting to bury your head in the sand and hope they go away, but that is not what positivity is all about. It is about looking squarely at problems without dwelling on them too much, with the determination to tackle anything that comes your way and manage your life in the best way you can.

284 Focus on solutions

The first step in dealing with a problem is to acknowledge and identify it, before trying to figure out a solution or find a way forward. Usually this is not a black-and-white process. There can be a lot of trial and error involved in problem solving. Embracing this in a realistic, determined way is part of positivity.

285 Find out about inspirational role models

Do some research into some of the gifted and famous people who have (or had) Aspergers (or where this is believed to be the case) and who manage to make wonderful contributions to the world even though they struggled with typical Asperger difficulties. Albert Einstein, for example, is believed to have had Asperger Syndrome, and had huge difficulties in managing his day-to-day life.

286 Remember that worrying is useless

The only time we are sure of is right now, this very moment, so we may as well enjoy it! Remember: 'The past is history, the future is mystery, this moment is a gift – that's why we call it present.'

11

When Things Go off the Rails

Depression
Challenging and destructive behaviour

No matter how well you do your parenting job, there are bound to be times when things go wrong. This chapter deals with:

- Depression (page 198)
- Challenging and destructive behaviour (page 204)

DEPRESSION

TIP BOX

Depression

287   Be vigilant
288   Make home a sanctuary
289   Encourage a healthy lifestyle
290   Exercise
291   Get a gym membership?
292   Establish routine
293   Encourage him to take pride in his personal appearance
294   Understand lazy days
295   Be there to lend an ear
296   Talk it through
297   Know when to stop talking
298   Recognise depression as a call to change
299   Encourage hobbies and pastimes
300   Get a pet
301   Help him find purpose
302   Think about other people
303   Get professional help

287 Be vigilant

Depression is a real risk for young people with Asperger Syndrome and it is a good idea to be vigilant about this, without of course being paranoid. Keep an eye out for clues. You know your child best and will have an intuitive sense of what to look out for.

You may notice in him an exaggeration of things you have seen before rather than anything completely new – more extreme withdrawal, mood swings, argumentativeness, aggression and so on. Or he may tell you himself that he is feeling depressed.

288 Make home a sanctuary

Prevention is better than cure, and if your child is happy in his home and family, and his relationship with you is a happy one, logic dictates that he will be less likely to become seriously depressed. But life is more complicated than that, of course, and, even with the most loving home and family life, there is no way to guarantee that your child will not go through a phase of depression at some point.

289 Encourage a healthy lifestyle

A healthy lifestyle is always a good idea, but if you think your child may be becoming depressed, this becomes a bigger, more urgent priority. Try to foster a healthy lifestyle in the home – healthy routines, diet, exercise and so forth.

Ultimately the aim is that he sees for himself the point of a healthy lifestyle and takes responsibility for creating his own, so discuss with him the benefits. Involve him and let him take responsibility as much as possible (meal planning, exercise regimes and so on).

290 Exercise

Exercise is arguably the world's number one anti-depressant, but when you are depressed it is often the last thing you feel like doing! If your child seems depressed and lethargic, encourage him to take some exercise and to incorporate exercise into his lifestyle. It doesn't need to be much initially, perhaps just a short walk to break the lethargy, get some fresh air and a change of scene. He might then agree a schedule to gradually increase the amount of exercise he does daily. Any type of exercise is beneficial, for example swimming, running or cycling – just whatever works for him.

291 Get a gym membership?

Consider a gym membership for a young person with AS, and possibly a suitable personal one-to-one trainer at least to get him started. The structure involved in a gym regime may appeal to him and the gym may actually turn out to be a valuable mental health tool.

292 Establish routine

Encourage your child to adopt healthy daily routines and rituals – without of course letting them turn into unhealthy obsessions and get out of balance.

293 Encourage him to take pride in his personal appearance

It is common to lose interest in your appearance when you are depressed. If you see this happening, encourage your child to at least take care of his personal grooming – shower, shaving and so on.

294 Understand lazy days

We all have lazy days from time to time. During lazy days we may want to lie in bed or on the sofa the whole day. And lazy days can serve a purpose, of course. It can be very comforting sometimes to lie about the house and let go of the stresses and pressures, or to know you have a lazy day to look forward to.

A problem only arises when there are too many lazy days. This can lead to depression in itself – or perhaps it is the other way round and too many lazy days can be a sign of depression. Either way, keep an eye on things and don't let lazy days get too out of balance. They may help your child feel better for a while, but don't encourage too many of them.

295 Be there to lend an ear

When we are depressed sometimes the thing we need most is just to know that someone else cares. Spend some time with your child, ideally one to one. Don't try to force him to talk, but be there as a listening ear if needs be.

296 Talk it through

It may be hard to know what to say to your child when he is depressed. Don't suggest solutions too hastily, because doing so can sound dismissive and simplistic. And he may not be ready to look for solutions. At this point he may just need to be heard. At one extreme you do not want to minimise his troubles. At the other extreme, you don't want to magnify things and make them seem worse than they are.

As well as listening and making sure he knows you are on his side (see also Tips 119–25), the best thing you can really do for him is to help him feel better about himself, perhaps by reminding him of his efforts and achievements and things you see as admirable about him (see also Tips 141–7).

And while you do not want to sound trite or use too many clichés, sometimes a few simple words chosen well and expressed sincerely can make all the difference:

'I hear what you are saying.'

'It's tough.'

'I hate to see you go through this kind of thing. You don't deserve to feel this way.'

'I know you will come through this.'

'I hope you feel better soon.'

'Please let me know if there is anything I can do to help.'

'Time heals all ills.'

'The darkest hour is before the dawn.'

297 Know when to stop talking

It is obviously better for your child to talk when he is depressed than to bottle things up. But sometimes talking goes too far and he can end up obsessed by his problems, and this can make the situation worse.

If you think this is happening, encourage him to stop talking about his problems for an agreed time. Explain the reason for this suggestion and reassure him that his problems are not being forgotten.

298 Recognise depression as a call to change

Depression is often best seen as a call to change. Talk to your child about this. Can he think of any changes which might improve his situation? Thinking about things this way can be empowering.

299 Encourage hobbies and pastimes

If your child has not already got an interesting and absorbing hobby, encourage him in this direction. If he used to have a passion or special interest, but has let this drop, encourage him to revisit it. He may have forgotten how much he enjoys it!

300 Get a pet

If your child likes animals, consider getting him a pet and encourage him to take good care of it.

301 Help him find purpose

'What's the point?' is a question often on the lips of adolescents. And it is also a question associated with depression.

Either way, aim to help him find a 'point' – something to become involved in which he sees as worthwhile, because purpose can be an excellent antidote to depression.

Ultimately in life he will need to find his own purpose, of course, and this may take time. For now, you can believe in him and encourage him to believe in himself and his future. He *has* a unique place and purpose in life and he will find it one day. In the meantime, searching for it is part of life's adventure.

302 Think about other people

When we are depressed we all tend to become wrapped up in ourselves. Encourage him to think about other people and their problems as well if you can.

303 Get professional help

Use your intuitive judgement as to when it is appropriate to seek professional help in respect of your child's depression, using the general rule of thumb that it is better to err on the side of caution and involve professionals too soon than not soon enough. His doctor should be able to offer help in the form of professional advice, reassurance, counselling, antidepressant medication and so on.

CHALLENGING AND DESTRUCTIVE BEHAVIOUR

TIP BOX

Challenging and destructive behaviour

304 Prevention is better than cure
305 Take extreme behaviour seriously
306 Work as a team
307 Investigate the reason
308 Don't add fuel to the fire
309 Use the 'When...then...' formula
310 Have the *lasting* word
311 Suggest a meeting
312 Look at options
313 Use a conch
314 Swap roles
315 Appeal to logic
316 Agree a way forward
317 Make it enforceable
318 Establish a crisis plan
319 Explain the role of external authorities
320 Don't make empty threats
321 Don't reward violence
322 Remove yourself
323 Try 'commando parenting'
324 Try tough love
325 Know when you've reached the last resort

304 Prevention is better than cure

It is of course far better to prevent extreme behaviour in the first place rather than deal with problems further down the line (see also Tip 116). But if you notice things starting to head off in the wrong direction, it is good to have a plan of action ready to deal with it. Here are some examples of challenging and destructive behaviour which qualify as extreme and need to be taken seriously:

- aggression
- self-harm
- alcohol and drug abuse
- problems with the law
- promiscuity
- running away
- squalor.

305 Take extreme behaviour seriously

Don't turn a blind eye or allow yourself to become gradually acclimatised to deteriorating standards of behaviour. Be very clear to your child about what you consider to be extreme behaviour: that, for example, using physical force is unacceptable.

306 Work as a team

When it comes to extreme behaviour, make sure the significant adults in your child's life are all on the same page. This is very important, so that he cannot play one person off against the other, and so that everyone concerned knows where they stand.

Make sure he gets a unified message about his behaviour and choices – particularly about standards, at what point his behaviour will be considered to have crossed the line, the consequences and any strategy to be used going forward.

307 Investigate the reason

When extreme behaviour starts to appear, put it at the very top of your list of priorities to be dealt with urgently.

Spend some time with your child as soon as possible; choose the right moment and tell him you are concerned about him, that you have noticed his behaviour deteriorating and you are anxious to find out whether there is a reason – and that if there is something wrong you would like to know in case you can do anything to help.

Encourage him to open up, and listen to what he has to say (see also Tips 176–85). If you cannot find out much from him directly, have a think about what is going on in his life which might be a factor. Have there been any significant changes recently? Is he associating with different people? Is he being bullied or set up in anyway (see also Tip 80)? Is he suffering from an underlying depression (see also Tips 287–303)?

308 Don't add fuel to the fire

In the heat of the moment try not to respond in anger and say things you will regret. It will probably just add fuel to the fire and make matters worse.

309 Use the 'When...then...' formula

In response to anger, try not to engage with your child at all until he has settled down and is speaking to you in a calm, respectful way. Use the 'When...then...' formula. For example, '*When* you have sat down and stopped shouting, *then* we can talk about this.'

Words are important and it is important in this formula to use 'when' rather than 'if'. The word 'when' works better because it has an air of authority and mastery, whereas 'if' introduces an element of uncertainty and gives him the misleading impression that he has a choice.

310 Have the *lasting* word

Try not to get drawn into protracted arguments and do not feel you have to 'win' by getting in the last word. Ultimately the important thing is that your word carries most weight. It doesn't matter who gets in the last word. What does matter is that you have the *lasting* word.

311 Suggest a meeting

When you are faced with an extreme behavioural issue, sometimes it makes more sense not to deal with it in the moment. Show that your concerns are serious by suggesting a meeting with all relevant parties at a later date and suggest that in the meantime the subject is dropped and that all involved think up some options for resolving the issues and going forward. The agreed date should not be too far in the future, but long enough away to let everyone concerned calm down and process the situation.

This approach has various advantages. Everyone should be more willing to let grievances and arguments drop temporarily when they know they will be addressed very soon. And it allows time for dust to settle, tempers to cool and all concerned to think more calmly and creatively about a way forward.

312 Look at options

Prepare for the meeting in whatever way you think appropriate. For example, investigate your child's grievances; talk to other people who might have a fresh perspective or helpful ideas to offer; make a list of options, pros and cons.

313 Use a conch

Start the meeting by taking it in turns to listen to what each other has to say. It can take a lot of patience and discipline to do this without interrupting each other. Perhaps you can keep the atmosphere light by using a 'conch'.

(A conch is any agreed object which has to be held by whoever is speaking at the time. Any person who is not holding the conch cannot speak till it is his turn to hold it. The conch can be any object you want it to be – even a banana if you like! See also Tip 181.)

314 Swap roles

Here is an interesting, challenging and useful exercise which can sometimes work very well, and which may appeal to the logical brain of a young person with AS.

After everyone has listened to each other's points of view, they swap roles to see how convincingly they can argue each other's viewpoint!

This technique can help in various ways:

- It can help clarify that people have heard and understood each other's point of view.

- It can help people get into each other's shoes and see each other's point of views.

- It can take the heat out of strongly held positions.

315 Appeal to logic

This is sometimes all it takes to bring about behaviour change in someone with AS. Helping your child see a logical reason for doing something is more likely to be effective than nagging. For example, my son smoked for a couple of years and like all smokers he was aware of the risks but chose to ignore them. But there was something about the logical approach of Allen Carr's (2011) book that helped him see clearly the reasons for not smoking and the most sensible way to stop. He read it through once and never smoked again!

316 Agree a way forward

Rather than impose solutions to behaviour problems, involve your child in discussion and planning. Take his suggestions seriously. Agree a way forward and a time for reviewing suggested solutions so you can both assess how well they are working and make changes if needs be.

317 Make it enforceable

Make sure any solutions you agree upon are realistic and enforceable.

318 Establish a crisis plan

If you have reason to anticipate extreme behaviour in the future, prepare a crisis plan and give your child appropriate warning.

319 Explain the role of external authorities

In serious cases of extreme behaviour, for example, involving violence, drug abuse and so on, let your child know that, unless the extreme behaviour is brought under control, you may consider it appropriate to involve external authorities, as a last resort. Tell him this in a matter-of-fact way and explain your reasons clearly, but not in an apologetic way.

Clarify what you would consider to be extreme enough behaviour to warrant the involvement of external authorities but that if it gets to that point the decision will be yours alone and there will be no point in him arguing.

State calmly that this option would be the last thing you would want, but that whether things end up there is up to him and how he decides to behave. If appropriate and, of course, only when the moment is right, consider submitting this understanding in writing, have him sign it and have it witnessed, to confirm that he has understood and to emphasise the seriousness of the situation.

320 Don't make empty threats

Let's take an extreme example. If your child has a drug habit and he has been funding his habit by stealing from you, tell him very clearly what the consequences will be if this ever happens again, and what your crisis plan is – and stick to it!

Your crisis plan in such an extreme situation might involve reporting him to the police, exposing him to the full force of the law and letting him take whatever legal procedure ensues. That is obviously an extreme position, which no parent will ever adopt lightly. Do not threaten something like this unless you really mean it, and do your best to make sure all the relevant adults in his life understand the reason and are 100 per cent on board.

You will also need to be sure that:

- your motivation is to help your child by forcing him to see reality and face consequences

- you have tried everything else you can think of to this end

- you are ready and prepared in practical terms to put the crisis plan into operation immediately if the circumstances arise (for example, you have relevant telephone numbers to hand, and you may have had informal discussion with the local police, so that they are already in the picture should they be called upon).

Remember, if you issue empty threats, your child will learn nothing – except that you do not mean what you say.

321 Don't reward violence

Never reward violence by giving in to it and letting your child have his way.

322 Remove yourself

Don't minimise extreme behaviour. If needs be, remove yourself and anyone else who might be in danger and be prepared to call on the authorities.

323 Try 'commando parenting'

In cases of very extreme behaviour, consider a period of 'commando parenting' (McGraw 2005) when *all* privileges (or close to all) are removed for a specified period of time. This may include all technology such as mobile phone, internet, music player, treat food and so on, and set a very clear and specific programme of behaviour as to how these privileges can be earned back.

Make sure your child is very clear on the distinction between entitlements and privileges and knows that you will not of course keep from him anything that he is entitled to. If necessary put this in writing in advance to prevent disputes.

324 Try tough love

When you are trying to change entrenched behaviour, don't be surprised if you get an extreme reaction. Things may get worse before they get better as your child tests the boundaries even harder than before. Hold firm and be strong and determined. He needs strong boundaries more than ever at this stage. Be prepared – there is a good chance that he will know how to push your buttons, and at some point you will feel cruel and guilty. Tough love can be tough on parents as well!

325 Know when you've reached the last resort

On a rare occasion, things can get so bad that there is nothing more you can usefully do and you may need to admit that you are out of your depth. Know when you have reached such a time and, if you are not certain, confide in someone whose opinion and discretion you trust or get a professional opinion. As a very last resort, call upon the appropriate authorities (social services, police and so on).

Tip Finder

A List of All the Ideas, Insights, Tips and Strategies in the Order That They Appear Throughout the Book

1. SOME THINGS NEVER CHANGE
Looking after yourself   PAGE

1. Keep your batteries charged up 17
2. Talking helps 18
3. Get support 18
4. Don't neglect other areas of your life 18
5. Worry less, plan more 19
6. Let yourself off the hook 19

2. UNDERSTANDING ASPERGER ADOLESCENCE
The work of understanding

7. Resolve to understand 26
8. Understanding takes time 27
9. Look at online resources and make contacts 27
10. Look close to home 27
11. Roll back the years 28
12. See AS as a signpost, not a label 28
13. Listen! 28
14. Encourage him to open up 29
15. Look within 29

16. Help him understand himself   30

17. Know the Seven Key Insights   30

18. Become a student   31

3. THE SEVEN KEY INSIGHTS
Key Insight # 1: Asperger extremes

19. Understand that he's 'like anyone else, only more so' . .   34

20. Recognise extremes and opposites: His individual profile   35

21. Adjust your expectations   36

22. Extremes can offer great learning opportunities   37

23. Direct his strengths   37

Key Insight # 2: Fish out of water

24. Be aware of a common thread   38

25. Look within: Understand being a fish out of water . . .   38

26. Encourage relationships that are likely to work   39

27. Identify people with common interests   39

28. Find like minds online   40

29. Rejoice in Asperger originality and differences   40

30. Listen with sensitivity   40

31. Find the right moment for listening   41

32. Don't minimise his feelings   41

33. Give him some perspective   42

34. Share and confide   43

Key Insight # 3: Rates of development

35. Set normal milestones to the side 44

36. Look within: Understand rates of development 45

37. Comparisons are odious! 45

38. Beware of jumping to conclusions. 46

39. Take a long view 46

40. Help him get a positive, realistic self-concept 47

41. Model late development in self 47

42. Validate and acknowledge progress 47

43. There's always another boat! 47

Key Insight # 4: Processing and sensory differences

44. Understand experiencing the world differently 49

45. Look within: Understand processing and
    sensory experiences 50

46. Don't jump to conclusions 52

47. Respect his need for solitude 52

48. Communicate clearly 52

49. Accept his preferred learning style. 53

50. Avoid TMI (too much information)! 53

51. Suggest scripts like 'Let me think'. 54

52. Try one to one 54

Key Insight # 5: Mind blindness

53. Understand mind reading 55

54. Look within: Understand mind blindness 56

55. Don't confuse mind blindness with immorality   56

56. Empathy works both ways   57

57. Translate the subtext   57

58. Explain the social rules   57

59. Nonverbal communication is hard to learn   57

60. Spell out 'the obvious'.   58

61. Encourage him to find ways to please   58

62. Be patient   58

63. Be aware of him feeling 'peopled out'.   59

64. Build up gradually from one to one   59

Key Insight # 6: Rigidity

65. Rigidity explains a lot!   60

66. Know that stubborn is a stubborn word   61

67. Consider trains versus cars   61

68. Look within: Understand rigidity in yourself   62

69. Be aware that change can be difficult   62

70. Don't mislead   62

71. Nobody can be good at everything   63

72. Encourage a healthy attitude to mistakes   63

73. Use some verbal tricks.   63

Key Insight # 7: Social vulnerability

74. Don't expect other people to get it   65

75. Recognise that it's a hidden disability   65

76. Social punishments can be very real   67

77. Keep an eye on the company he keeps. 67

78. Make sure he is aware of danger 67

79. Be vigilant 68

80. Be prepared in case bullying occurs 68

81. Help him learn the Social Curriculum 69

82. Don't take things personally 69

83. Never leave him friendless. 70

84. Appreciate the value of friends and family. 70

85. Don't let him get 'peopled out' 70

4. THE BEST APPROACH
Being calm and assertive

86. Recognise the value of a calm and assertive approach . . 74

87. Be relaxed. 74

88. Explain consequences calmly 75

89. Use fewer words. 75

90. When you lose your temper you have lost. 75

Parenting with confidence

91. Parent with confidence 76

92. Have faith in yourself 77

93. Fake it till you make it 78

94. Use humour 79

Being pragmatic

95. Do what works 80

96. Agree rather than impose 80

97. Know you can't deal with everything at once 82

98. Cultivate patience 83

99. Reserve your opinion 83

100. Go along with things 83

101. Understand that timing is everything 83

Encouraging motivation

102. Understand his agenda 85

103. Believe in him. 85

104. Help him see the point 86

105. Use the project approach 86

106. Get him on the train 86

107. Offer limited reassurance 87

108. Find the ideal motivator 87

Avoiding conflict

109. Model harmony 88

110. Choose your battles carefully 88

111. ACT. 89

112. Spell it out 89

113. Involve him 90

114. Guard the line in the sand. 90

115. Use scripts, affirmations and sound bites. 91

116. Nip it in the bud 92

117. Be in it to win it. 92

118. Recognise what not to do in the heat of the moment . . 93

5. YOUR RELATIONSHIP WITH YOUR CHILD
Being on the same side

119. Let it be beyond doubt 96

120. Tell him in words 96

121. Believe in him. 97

122. Side with him, not his behaviour 97

123. Confide and identify 98

124. Treat confidences with respect. 99

125. Recognise that falling out is not a problem 99

Giving him the benefit of the doubt

126. He is probably unaware of how he comes across 100

127. He usually does not intend to cause offence. 101

128. He usually wants to get it right 101

129. 'The obvious' is not always so obvious! 102

Mutual respect

130. It starts with self-respect 104

131. It's for his sake too 105

132. Meet him where he is at. 105

133. It's the little things that count. 105

134. Discuss earning respect 105

135. 'If it matters to you...'. 106

136. Respect his decisions 106

137. Keep your word. 106

138. Step back 107

139. Respect his passion 107

140. Support his dreams and visions 107

6. SELF-IMAGE
Encourage him to have a positive self-regard

141. Remember Lily's secret 110

142. Be proud of him – and make sure he knows it! 111

143. Look for opportunities 112

144. Recognise the power of praise. 112

145. Use the past tense method. 112

146. Use the positive sandwich technique 113

147. Change is possible 113

Encourage him to have a positive attitude to Asperger Syndrome

148. Encourage him to be Aspie and proud of it! 114

149. Your attitude matters 114

150. Examine your attitude to AS. 115

151. Develop an appreciation for AS 116

152. Explore the positives 116

153. Remember that Aspies are not boring!. 116

154. Encourage positive role models 117

155. Let AS help you learn about yourself 117

156. Encourage a fair press. 117

Help shape core beliefs

157. Plant seeds 118

158. Make words matter 119

159. Take a 'no strings' approach. 120

160. Nobody can be good at everything!. 120

161. Explain the jagged profile 120

162. Emphasise that mistakes are for learning 121

163. Encourage him to play to his strengths 121

164. Tell him you've noticed the effort he is making 121

165. Practise 'holding a mirror' up to each other 121

166. Give the gift of time. 122

167. Take an interest in his interests 122

168. Say that you enjoy his company. 122

169. Tell him that you cherish his individuality. 122

170. Create happy memories 123

171. Let him know that you want his input. 123

172. Tell him you will be sensitive 123

173. Let him know that he can make changes 123

174. Confidence comes in baby steps. 123

175. His future is full of hope 124

7. COMMUNICATION THAT WORKS
Ready to listen, ready to talk

176. Make one-to-one time. 126

177. Communication can't be forced 126

178. Make friends before you make points 127

179. Think quantity then quality 127

180. Don't be put off. 127

181. Talk to him, not at him 128

182. Agree to turn phones off 129

183. Don't pry 129

184. Say 'Tell me more about that' 129

185. Be there 130

Clear, honest and direct communication

186. Spell things out 131

187. Make expectations clear 131

188. C and R (Clarify and Repeat) 132

189. Don't overload 132

190. Be calm and logical 132

191. Use humour carefully 133

192. Don't be a know-it-all 133

193. Don't pretend to be perfect 133

194. Help him to understand socially acceptable lies 133

195. Love without honesty. 135

8. A PREDICTABLE WORLD?
Understanding control versus chaos

196. Learn about the systemising brain. 138

197. Understand control and chaos. 139

198. Find out about Asperger life coaching. 139

199. Recognise difficulties coming to light 140

200. Minimise uncertainty 140

201. Let go of control 140

202. Understand MOB – The focus 141

203. Understand MOB – The benefits 141

204. Make sense of The Problem with People 141

Encouraging order and structure

205. Encourage him to structure his own life 142

206. Help him see the point 143

207. Make use of technology. 144

208. Understand 'executive function'. 145

209. Use SMART goals. 145

210. Write it down 145

211. Use prompts and reminders 146

212. Send a message!. 146

213. Try mind mapping 146

214. Find the right life coach. 146

215. Nurture healthy traditions or routines 146

216. Create your own routines 147

Setting boundaries and limits

217. Overindulgence is a mistake. 148

218. Agree basic ground rules 149

219. Create a written contract 150

220. Rules without relationship mean rebellion. 150

221. Draw a clear line in the sand 150

222. Be fair, give clear consequences 151

223. Explain entitlement versus privilege 151

9. THE PROBLEM WITH PEOPLE
The Social Curriculum

224. Understand social heaven and hell 154

225. It's the hardest subject of all. 156

226. To learn is to grow 158

227. Help him understand the social game 158

228. There's more than one right answer 159

229. Help him see the point 159

230. It's like learning to swim 160

231. Break it down. 161

232. Analyse social behaviour 163

233. Start in the shallow pool 163

234. Approach it like coaching sessions 164

235. Reflect and rehearse 164

236. Try using scripts. 165

237. It's the thought that counts 166

238. Use compliments 166

239. Help him make amends 166

240. Great conversationalists can be very quiet!. 166

Emotions and nonverbal communication

241. It's like a foreign language to Aspies 167

242. Help him fill in the gaps. 168

243. Explain social masks 168

244. Translate intentions 169

245. Verbalise the rules. 169

246. Mute it 170

247. Help him understand that hierarchies matter 170

248. Understand emotions in context. 171

249. Name feelings. 171

250. 'It's not unusual'. 172

251. You're not the only one 172

252. Spell out the impact. 173

253. Understand responsibility versus guilt. 173

254. It's good to talk. 173

255. Solitude can help 174

Positive social experiences

256. Time alone – whose problem is it? 175

257. Agree limits on solitary activities 175

258. One man's meat is another man's poison 176

259. Be selective 177

260. Think of alternatives to small talk. 178

261. Discuss romantic and sexual relationships? 178

262. Realise that online relationships matter 178

263. Challenge your attitude 179

264. Be careful with the internet 179

10. PREPARATION FOR ADULTHOOD
Encouraging self-awareness and responsibility

265. Show him how to 'know thyself' 182

266. Encourage his self-awareness and maturity 182

267. Understand that mirrors are voluntary. 183

268. Build his Asperger awareness 184

269. Give him his say. 184

270. Recognise his profile of extremes 185

271. Discuss the 'facts of life'. 185

272. Talk about romance and primary relationships? 187

Thinking about college and career

273. Consider continuing education?. 189

274. Notify future employers and educators? 190

275. Identify levels of support 191

276. Find extra assistance. 191

277. Get off on the right foot 192

278. Establish agreed contact times. 193

279. Be vigilant 193

Encouraging a positive outlook

280. It's a matter of choice 194

281. Encourage positivity. 195

282. 'Always look on the bright side'. 195

283. Acknowledge problems 195

284. Focus on solutions. 195

285. Find out about inspirational role models 196

286. Remember that worrying is useless 196

11. WHEN THINGS GO OFF THE RAILS
Depression

287. Be vigilant 198

288. Make home a sanctuary 199

289. Encourage a healthy lifestyle 199

290. Exercise 199

291. Get a gym membership? 200

292. Establish routine 200

293. Encourage him to take pride in his personal appearance 200

294. Understand lazy days 200

295. Be there to lend an ear 201

296. Talk it through 201

297. Know when to stop talking 202

298. Recognise depression as a call to change 202

299. Encourage hobbies and pastimes 202

300. Get a pet 202

301. Help him find purpose 203

302. Think about other people 203

303. Get professional help 203

Challenging and destructive behaviour

304. Prevention is better than cure 204

305. Take extreme behaviour seriously 205

306. Work as a team 205

307. Investigate the reason 206

308. Don't add fuel to the fire 206

309. Use the 'When…then…' formula 206

310. Have the *lasting* word 207

311. Suggest a meeting 207

312. Look at options 207

313. Use a conch 208

314. Swap roles 208

315. Appeal to logic 208

316. Agree a way forward 209

317. Make it enforceable 209

318. Establish a crisis plan 209

319. Explain the role of external authorities 209

320. Don't make empty threats 210

321. Don't reward violence 211

322. Remove yourself 211

323. Try 'commando parenting' 211

324. Try tough love 211

325. Know when you've reached the last resort 212

Useful Websites

Asperger Life Coaching

www.aspergerlifecoaching.com

Information and advice on life coaching for people affected by Asperger Syndrome.

Asperger-Syndrome.me.uk

www.asperger-syndrome.me.uk

Offering help, support and information regarding Asperger Syndrome.

Autism NI

www.autismni.org

Website of Autism NI, Northern Ireland's leading autism charity.

Bullying UK

www.bullying.co.uk

For information and advice on bullying.

College Autism Spectrum

www.collegeautismspectrum.com

For information and advice relating to preparation for and life at college or university.

Coping: A Survival Guide for People with Asperger Syndrome

www-users.cs.york.ac.uk/alistair/survival/index.html

Website dedicated to Marc Segar, a young person with Asperger Syndrome who died tragically in a road traffic accident in 1997, and whose writing has been deeply helpful and influential.

Improve Your Social Skills

www.improveyoursocialskills.com

A comprehensive online guide to social skills, written by an Aspie for Aspies, with 50 lessons covering topics such as body language and conversation.

National Autistic Society

www.autism.org.uk

Website of the National Autistic Society in the UK.

NHS Choices

www.nhs.uk/Conditions/Depression/Pages/Introduction.aspx

Information about depression from the National Health Service.

Optimnem Foreign Language Courses

www.optimnem.co.uk

Foreign language courses offered by Daniel Tammett, an individual with Asperger Syndrome.

UK Safer Internet Centre

www.saferinternet.org.uk

For good advice on safe use and supervision of the internet.

Wrong Planet

www.wrongplanet.net

Web community for people affected by ASD (autistic spectrum disorders).

Bibliography

Attwood, T. (1998) *Asperger's Syndrome: A Guide for Parents and Professionals.* London: Jessica Kingsley Publishers.

Attwood, T. (2006a) 'Asperger's Syndrome: Educational placements for children with Asperger's Syndrome.' NSW, Australia: Learning Links. Available at www.learninglinks.org.au/pdf/infosheets/LLIS%2027_Aspergers.pdf, accessed on 13 July 2013.

Attwood, T. (2006b) *The Complete Guide to Asperger's Syndrome.* London: Jessica Kingsley Publishers.

Attwood, T. (2013) 'The pattern of abilities and development of girls with Asperger's Syndrome.' Available at www.tonyattwood.com.au/index.php?Itemid=181&catid=45:archived-resource-papers&id=80:the-pattern-of-abilities-and-development-of-girls-with-aspergers-syndrome&option=com_content&view=article, accessed on 13 July 2013.

Baron-Cohen, S. (2002) 'The extreme male brain theory of autism.' *Trends in Cognitive Sciences 6,* 248–254.

Baron-Cohen, S. (2003) *The Essential Difference.* Harmondsworth: Penguin.

Baron-Cohen, S., Tager-Flusberg, H. and Cohen, D.J. (1993) *Understanding Other Minds: Perspectives from Autism.* Oxford: Oxford University Press.

Bissonnette, B. (2013) *Asperger's Syndrome Workplace Survival Guide: A Neurotypical's Secrets for Success.* London: Jessica Kingsley Publishers.

Boyd, B. (2003) *Parenting a Child with Asperger Syndrome.* London: Jessica Kingsley Publishers.

Brian, D. (1996) *Einstein: A Life.* New York: John Wiley.

Carr, A. (2011) *Stop Smoking.* London: Arcturus Publishing.

Dubin, N. (2009) *Asperger Syndrome and Anxiety: A Guide to Successful Stress Management.* London: Jessica Kingsley Publishers.

Faber, A. and Mazlish, E. (1982) *How to Talk So Kids Will Listen and Listen So Kids Will Talk.* London: Piccadilly Press.

Gardner, H. (1993) *Frames of Mind: The Theory of Multiple Intelligences.* London: Fontana.

Garland, R. (1991) 'Juvenile delinquency in the Graeco-Roman world.' *History Today 41,* 10. Available at www.historytoday.com/robert-garland/juvenile-delinquency-graeco-roman-world, accessed on 11 July 2013.

Golding, W. (2012[1954]) *Lord of the Flies.* London: Faber and Faber.

Goleman, D. (1996) *Emotional Intelligence.* London: Bloomsbury.

Grandin, T. (2002) 'The world needs people with Asperger's syndrome.' Cerebrum. Available at www.dana.org/news/cerebrum/detail.aspx?id=2312, accessed on 12 July 2013.

Grandin, T. (2005) *The Unwritten Rules of Social Relationships.* London: Future Horizons.

Lane, M. (2004) 'What Asperger's syndrome has done for us.' *BBC News Online Magazine.* Available at http://news.bbc.co.uk/1/hi/3766697.stm, accessed on 12 July 2013.

Makin, P.E. and Lindley, P. (1991) *Positive Stress Management.* London: Kogan Page.

Matthews, D. (2009) 'Discipline: The power of praise.' Available at www.examiner.com/article/discipline-the-power-of-praise, accessed on 13 July 2013.

McGraw, P. (2005) *The Family First Workbook: Specific Tools, Strategies and Skills for Creating a Phenomenal Family.* New York: Free Press.

National Autistic Society (2013a) 'Befriending and mentoring.' Available at www.autism.org.uk/befriending, accessed on 13 July 2013.

National Autistic Society (2013b) 'Courses for professionals in autism and other related topics.' Available at www.autism.org.uk/working-with/training-and-experience/courses-for-professionals-in-autism-and-other-related-topics.aspx, accessed on 11 July 2013.

National Autistic Society (2013c) 'Social groups.' Available at www.autism.org.uk/our-services/residential-community-and-social-support/social-support/social-groups.aspx, accessed on 14 July 2013.

Nierenberg, G. and Calero, H. (1980) *How to Read a Person Like a Book.* London: Thorsons.

O'Neill, J.L (eds) (1999) *Through The Eyes of Aliens: A Book About Autistic People.* London: Jessica Kingsley Publishers.

Patrick, N.J. (2002) *Social Skills for Teenagers and Adults with Asperger Syndrome.* London: Jessica Kingsley Publishers.

Stanford, A. (2002) *Asperger Syndrome and Long-term Relationships.* London: Jessica Kingsley Publishers.

Willey, L.H. (1999) *Pretending to be Normal: Living with Asperger's Syndrome.* London: Jessica Kingsley Publishers.

Index

abrasive manners 101, 128
abuse
    drug 205, 209
    against yourself 90–1
academic performance 66, 140, 189
accomplishments, listing your own 77
ACT acronym, for avoiding conflict 89
action plans 204
adolescence, recalling your own 28, 29–30,
    171
adulthood, preparation for 181–95
advice
    professional 203
    reserving 83
    on romantic relationships 187–8
    taking from your child 123
affirmations, in conflict situations 91
aggression
    difference between assertiveness and 90
    your child being aggressive 198, 205
alcohol
    abuse 205
    awareness of dangers of 67–8
alienation 38–9, 41, 43
allowances, making 24
anger, responding to 206–7
    see also heat of the moment
anxiety 62, 141
apologizing 162, 166
appearance, taking a pride in personal 200
approximations, socially acceptable 134
arguments 63–4, 75, 81, 198, 207
arrogance 36, 46, 100
AS (Asperger Syndrome)
    adjusting to diagnosis of 84
    causes of 27
    encouraging a positive attitude 114–17
    as a hidden disability 24, 56, 65–7, 156

individual profiles of 35–6
    learning about 77–8
    notifying people about 190–1
Asperger extremes 30, 34–7, 45, 53, 64, 66,
    85, 117, 127, 133, 139, 143, 185
Asperger groups 27, 177
Asperger traits
    positive aspects 116
    in yourself and family members 25, 27, 35,
    115, 117
assertive, being 74–5, 90
attention
    paying 40–1, 41–2, 50, 51, 84
    withholding 92
attention-seeking behaviour 66
Attwood, T. 66, 68, 171
auditory learning 53
authorities, involvement of external 209–10,
    211, 212
authority
    problems relating to those in 66
    teaching concept of 133, 170–1
Autism Quizzes 117
automatic, actions becoming 157, 161
autonomy 22, 81, 106

bad company, awareness of dangers of 67–8
bad habits, stopping 92, 204
bad news, breaking 135
Baron-Cohen, S. 138
befrienders 70
behavioural contracts 90, 150, 210
being there 28, 130, 187, 201
belief
    in your child 12, 85–6, 97, 124, 203
    your child's self- 124, 203
    in yourself 77–8
beliefs, shaping core 118–24

benefit of the doubt, giving your child the 100–3
blind eye
   not turning a 90, 205
   turning a 75, 83, 88–9
bluntness 32, 128
body language 55, 170
boring
   being considered 69, 127
   people with AS are not 116
boundaries 75, 89–90, 148–51, 211–12
Boyd, B. 15
brain, Asperger brain as systemising 138, 139
bullying 67, 68–9, 169, 193, 206
   being bullied by your child 104
burn out, avoiding 17–18

calendars, on mobile phones 144
Calero, H. 170
calm, being 74–5, 78–9, 132, 171–2
calming measures 52
capability 46, 52, 100, 123, 158
Carr, A. 209
causes of AS 27
challenging and destructive behaviour 204–12
change
   dealing with 83–4
   encouraging 113, 123, 158, 202
   resistance to 60, 62
chaos, versus control 138–41
clarify and repeat technique 132
clarity, importance of 40–1, 52, 58, 62–3, 131
clocks, on mobile phones 144
college, thinking about 189–93
comfort zone, stepping out of 124
'commando parenting' 211
communication, clear, honest and direct 131–5
company, keeping an eye on 67, 68
comparisons, not making 45–6
compliments, socially acceptable 134, 164, 166
computers, making use of 144–5
   see also internet
'conch shells', using 128–9, 208
conclusions, not jumping to 46, 52, 100, 169
confidence
   having 76, 78–9, 123–4
   losing 45–6, 59, 66, 76, 123

   parenting with 76–9
confidences, respecting 98, 99
confiding, in your child 43, 63, 98
conflict, avoiding 88–94
consequences, explaining 75, 89–90, 151, 210
contraception 186
contracts, behavioural 90, 150, 210
control, versus chaos 138–41
controlling behaviour
   avoiding yourself 80, 82, 106–7, 140
   in your child 31, 61, 143
conventions
   being unaware of social 102–3, 170
   rejecting 36, 147
conversationalists 166
coping mechanisms 24, 27
core beliefs, shaping 118–24
correction, resistance to 60
counselling 115, 203
counter-productive behaviour 29, 144, 150, 160
crisis plans 209, 210
criticism
   'holding a mirror' up technique 121–2, 183–4
   positive sandwich technique 113
   resistance to 60
cruel
   not being cruel yourself 93, 119
   your child making you feel 212

danger
   awareness of 67–8, 97, 169, 178, 211
   online 40, 179–80
'dating game' 187
decision-making
   difficulties with 60, 85–6
   encouraging 64, 81–2
   respecting decisions 106
deluded, being 46
depression 198–203
   causes of 67, 68
   and extreme behaviour 206
   need for vigilance 68, 175, 176, 198
destiny, mastery of 124
destructive and challenging behaviour 204–12
development issues 31, 44–8, 120
diagnosis of AS, adjusting to 84
dialogue, importance of 128–9, 179

difference, respecting 40
differences
    processing and sensory 31, 49–54
    resolving 99, 127
dignity
    being treated with yourself 90
    respecting your child's 178
diplomatic, being 160
directness 32, 128, 131
disobedience, dealing with 93
documentary technique 78
dogmatism 31, 61
dominance, need for *see* controlling behaviour
'don't care' attitude 172
dreams, supporting 107
drugs, issues around 67–8, 205, 210

education, continuing 189–93
    see also learning
effort, noticing 121, 124, 201
Einstein, Albert 196
'elephants in the room', ignoring 134
email, as an aid to memory 146
embarrassment 45, 123, 186, 1115
emotional development 44
emotions, teaching about 141, 171–4
empathy
    encouraging 57
    lack of 56, 173
entitlement, versus privilege 151, 211
euphemisms 134
exaggeration 57
exams, revision methods 53
executive function 50, 51, 145
exercise, benefits of 199
expectations
    adjusting 36–7
    making clear 131
    unrealistic 151
extreme behaviour 204–12
extremes, Asperger 30, 34–7, 45, 53, 64, 66,
    85, 117, 127, 133, 139, 143, 185

'facts of life', discussing 185–7
failure 36, 100, 124, 158
faith
    in yourself 77–8
    see also belief
false promises 63
family, creating a happy 199
family members
    Asperger traits in 27, 117

modelling behaviour on 105
    support from 70
fear, overcoming 163
feedback, giving 112, 132, 164
feelings 41–2, 42–3, 171–2
financial support 18
fish out of water, being a 30, 38–43
flexibility issues 31, 47, 62, 143
focus, retaining 50, 51
food preferences 51
forgiveness 23, 99, 162
frustration, causes of 51, 130

gap years 190
Garland, R. 22
genetics 27
gifts, giving 166
girls, sexual naivety of 57, 67
Golding, W., *Lord of the Flies* 128
Grandin, T. 40
ground rules, setting 149–50
guilt
    feeling yourself 212
    versus responsibility 173
gym membership 200

happiness
    creating happy memories 123
    making someone else happy 58
harmony 88, 127
healthy lifestyle, encouraging a 199
heat of the moment
    taking the heat out of the 78, 79, 91–2
    what not to do in the 75, 93–4, 98,
        119–20, 206
hidden disability, AS as a 24, 56, 65–7, 156
hierarchies, understanding 170–1
hobbies 18, 142, 202
home, creating a happy 199
honesty 63, 98, 126, 131, 133, 134, 135
hope, future is full of 124
hormonal changes 62, 172
hugs, importance of 111
humiliation 51, 67, 93, 123
humour, use of 79, 133, 176
hyper sensitivity 49
hypo sensitivity 49

ideas, planting seeds of 63, 118–19, 172,
    184
imagination, exercise in 64

immorality, not to be confused with mind
     blindness 56
impact, of choices and behaviour 173, 182–3
individual profiles of AS 35–6
information processing *see* processing and
     sensory differences
insecurity 75, 76
intentions, translating 57, 66, 168, 169
interest, showing an 40–1, 41–2, 106
interests
     sharing 39, 42, 122
     special 50, 85, 107, 202
internet
     dangers of 40, 179–80
     UK Safer Internet Centre 40, 42
     uses of 18, 27, 40, 178–9
interrupting, not 40–1, 208
interviews 66, 192
intuition 58, 198, 203
isolation 40–1, 67, 174, 176

jobs, holding down 71
judgement
     being judged 67, 100
     errors of 66, 67

key insights 30–1, 33–71
     Asperger extremes 30, 34–7
     fish out of water 30, 38–43
     mind blindness 31, 55–9
     processing and sensory differences 31,
          49–54
     rates of development 31, 44–8
     rigidity 31, 60–4
     social vulnerability 31, 65–71
knee jerk reactions *see* heat of the moment
knowledge, not knowing everything 133

Lane, M. 38
last resort, knowing when have reached the
     212
law, problems with the 205
lazy days, understanding 200
learning
     about AS 77–8
     adult 48
     further education 189–93
     life-long 46, 120
     modelling 47
     positive attitude to 158
     styles 24, 50, 51, 53
lethargy 199, 200
letting some things go 36, 75, 83, 140, 144

lies, socially acceptable 57, 133–4
life coaching 51, 139–40, 146
limits *see* boundaries
lines, crossing 89, 90, 90–1, 150–1, 205
listening
     being ready to listen 126–30
     finding the right moment for 41, 144
     importance of 28–9, 40–1, 43, 68, 132,
          173–4, 184–5, 201, 206
literal, taking words literally 98, 133, 169
logical, being 57, 67, 81, 86, 102, 103, 132,
          144, 151, 159, 208–9
loneliness 21, 39, 40–1, 41, 42
looking after yourself 17–19
looking within
     being a fish out of water 38–9
     mind blindness 56
     processing and sensory experiences 50–1
     rates of development 45
     reasons for 29–30
     rigidity 62
love
     and honesty 135
     importance of 110–11
     tough 211–12
     unconditional 15–16, 120

massages, for relaxation 74
Matthews, D. 87
McGraw, P. 211
meanness 102, 158, 160
meditation 74
meetings, about extreme behaviour 207–8
memory
     idiosyncratic 50, 103
     selective 51
     writing as an aid to 145
mind blindness 31, 55–9
mind mapping software 146
mirroring 159
mirrors, 'holding a mirror' up technique
          121–2, 183–4
misleading, being 62–3
mistakes
     encouraging a healthy attitude to 63
     learning from 106, 121
     making 100, 120
MOB (Moderation, Order and Balance) focus
          141
mobile phones
     making use of 144–5
     turning off 129

mood swings 62, 198
moral issues 56, 170, 186
motivation, encouraging 85–7
mute it exercise 170
mutual support, importance of 18, 34–5

naivety
    sexual 57, 67
    social 100
National Autistic Society 18, 70, 177
neutral tone of voice, keeping a 78
nice, being 160
Nierenberg, G. 170
'no', saying 149
nonverbal communication 49, 51, 55–6,
        57–8, 58–9, 141, 167–71
notifying people about AS 190–1

obsessions 60, 61, 85, 141, 174, 202
obvious, not recognizing the 40–1, 58, 86,
        96–7, 100–1, 102–3, 131, 168
offence issues 69–70, 100, 101, 134
one-to-one communication 54, 59, 126, 127,
        201
online relationships 178–9
Open University 48
opening up, encouraging 28, 29, 126, 206
order
    craving for 60
    encouraging a healthy level of 62, 142–7
organisational skills 50, 139
originality, respecting 40, 116, 122, 185
over-protective, being 106–7
overbearing, being 61, 127
overindulgence, avoiding 148–9
overwhelmed, being 59, 70–1

parenting
    being pragmatic 80–4
    with confidence 76–9
past tense method of praise 112–13
pastimes 18, 142, 202
patience, importance of 58–9, 83, 144
patronising, appearing 16, 87, 105, 111
peer groups
    as bad company 67
    lack of 22, 39, 62
'peopled out', being 59, 70–1
perfectionism 60, 63, 100, 101–2
nobody is perfect 19, 97, 133, 162
personal appearance, taking a pride in 200
personal trainers 200

personally, not taking things 69–70
persuasion 75, 144
pets, caring for 202
phobias, overcoming 163
phones, turning off 129
physical changes 43, 62
physical force 69, 205
planting seeds of ideas 63, 118–19, 172, 184
pleasing, encouraging 58
PMI (plus, minus, interesting) lists 64
point, your child not seeing the point of 86,
        143–4, 159–60, 176, 203
point of view
    seeing another's 57, 63, 64, 106, 173, 208
    seeing from your child's 176
polar extremes verbal trick 64
police, involving 210
pornography, online 180
positive attitude to AS, encouraging a 114–17
positive outlook, encouraging a 194–6
positive sandwich technique 113
pragmatism 80–4
praise, power of 87, 112–13, 201
prayer 74
predictability 23, 60
presents 58, 166
pressure 83–4, 145
pride 111–12, 114
prioritization 82
privilege, versus entitlement 151, 211
problems
    acknowledging 195
    confiding with your child 98
    resolving 99, 127, 195–6, 209
    stopping talking about 202
    thinking about others' 203
processing and sensory differences 31, 49–54
processing overload 50, 51, 53, 132
processing speed 50, 51, 52, 84
procrastination 89, 90
professional help, for depression 203
profiles, individual profiles of AS 35–6
progress, validating and acknowledging 47
projects, seeing through 50, 86, 145
promiscuity 67, 205
promises
    false 63
    keeping 106
prompts, visual 146
prying, not to pry 129, 165

quality time 127
quiet, being 126

rates of development 31, 44–8
reading, for relaxation 74
reality, protection from 149
rebelliousness 66, 81, 106, 142, 150
record-keeping, for bullying 69
reflection, after social events 165
rehearsing social situations 164–5
relationships
    circles of 154–5
    importance of 156
    main components of 162–3
    online 178–9
    parent–child 43, 95–107
        being on the same side 96–9
        giving him the benefit of the doubt 100–3
        mutual respect 104–7
    romantic 178, 187–8
    sexual 178
relaxation techniques 74
reminders, visual 146
repetition 41–2, 53, 132
rescue phrases 165
resentment 150
respect
    being treated with yourself 90
    mutual 104–7
    treating others with 160, 172–3
    treating your child with 99
responsibility, encouraging 182–8
responsibility versus guilt 173
revision methods 53
reward schemes 87, 129
ridicule 66, 67
right, need to be 60, 62
rigidity 31, 60–4
rituals 61, 200
role models 196
role play 164
role swapping 208
romantic relationships 178, 187–8
routine
    craving for 60, 143
    hostility to 143
routines 61, 142–3, 146–7, 147, 200
rude, appearing 69, 92,100,102, 110
rules
    setting 149–50
    unwritten social 163, 165–6, 169–70, 187
running away 205

safe, keeping yourself 211
Safer Internet Centre, UK 40, 42
sarcasm 79, 93, 133
schedules, on mobile phones 144
school, underachievement at 47–8
scripts 54, 79, 91, 129–30, 165, 201–2
secretive behaviour 129
seeds, planting seeds of ideas 63, 118–19,
    172, 184
self-awareness 25, 30, 47, 49–50, 159,
    182–8
    see also key insights
self-esteem
    benefits of positive 111
    diminishing 45–6, 112, 120
    enhancing 81, 112
self-harm 205
self-image 109–24
self-respect 104
sensitivity
    hyper 49
    hypo 49
    listening with 40–1
    to situations 123
sensory differences 31, 39, 49–54
sensory input 51
sex
    awareness of dangers of 67–8
    discussing the 'facts of life' 185–7
sexual naivety 57, 67
sexual relationships, whether to discuss 178
sexually transmitted diseases 186
sharing
    interests 39, 42
    own stories 43
shortcomings, confiding your own 63
side, being on your child's side 96–9, 201
silences 127
sleeping problems, causes of 68
small talk 58, 164, 178
SMART (Smart, Measurable, Achievable,
    Realistic and Time-based) goals 145
smoking, stopping 208–9
social behaviour, analyzing your own 163
social conventions see Social Curriculum
Social Curriculum 58–9, 69, 102–3, 133–4,
    141, 154–66, 187
social development 44, 154–6
social experiences, positive 175–80
social masks 168–9
social maturity, delay in 66
social media 40

social punishments 67
social rules, explaining 57, 165
social situations, your own experiences 51
social vulnerability 31, 56, 57, 65–71, 100
socialising, with other Aspies 177
solitude
    agreeing limits on solitary activities 175–6
    respecting need for 52, 71, 174, 175, 192
sound bites, in conflict situations 91–2
space, need for 52
speaking in turn 128–9, 208
special events, your child's attitude towards 177
special interests 50
spoiling, avoiding 149
spontaneity, lack of 83
squalor 205
standards, maintaining 151, 205
stories, sharing your own 43
strengths
    acknowledging your own 133
    directing 37
    making the most of 121
stress 62, 83, 91, 131, 161
structure, encouraging 62, 142–7
stubbornness 31, 61
students, parents as 31–2, 37, 47
subtexts, translating 57, 66, 168, 169
Sudoko 178
summarising 53
support
    financial and practical 18
    identifying levels of 191–2, 193
    importance of mutual 18, 34
support groups 18, 27, 34–5, 177
systemising, Asperger brain as 138, 139

taboos, between parents and children 178, 185
talking
    being ready to talk 126–30
    extent to which your child talks 127–8
    importance for parents 18
    importance for people with AS 29, 173–4
    knowing when to stop 202
    letting people talk about themselves 166
    talking things through 140
    to your child about respect 105–6
tasks, seeing through 50, 86, 145
teamwork 160, 205

technology, making use of 144–5
television
    turning off 129
    watching on mute 170
temper, losing your own 75
texting, as an aid to memory 146
thinking time 132
threats, not making empty 210–11
time
    as a healer 171, 202
    quality time 122, 127
timing, importance of 80, 83–4, 144
tone of voice, keeping neutral 78
tough love 211–12
train analogy 86
train track analogy 61
truth-telling 57
TV
    turning off 129
    watching on mute 170

uncertainty
    dislike of 60
    minimising 140
underachievement 47–8
understanding adolescents 21–32
    benefits 23–5
    importance of 21–3
    tips 26–32
undesirable behaviour, stopping 92, 151, 204
unhappiness, inability to express 101
unreasonableness 31, 61
    countering 63–4

verbal tricks 63–4
views, respecting another's 57, 63, 64, 106
violence
    not rewarding 211
    against yourself 90–1
visions, supporting 107
visual prompts and reminders 53, 146
vulnerability see social vulnerability

weaknesses, acknowledging your own 133
'When…then…' formula 206–7
white lies 57, 133–4
wilfulness 61
'winning' conflicts 92–3, 150, 195, 207
withdrawn, being 126, 130, 198

words
    importance of right 206–7
    taking literally 98, 133, 169
    telling your child in 96–7, 97–8, 119–20,
        168
    using fewer 75
work issues 61, 145, 189–93
worrying 19, 196
writing
    as an aid to memory 145
    putting decisions in 90, 150, 210
Wrong Planet website 43

yoga 74
yourself, looking after 17–19